Graduate School and Beyond

Graduate School and Beyond

Earning and Using Your Advanced Degree

Mark H. Rossman, EdD
Professor Emeritus
Capella University

Paradigm Publishers
Boulder • London

Published in the United States by Paradigm Publishers, 2845 Wilderness Place, Suite 200, Boulder, CO 80301 USA.

Paradigm Publishers is the trade name of Birkenkamp & Company, LLC, Dean Birkenkamp, President and Publisher.

Library of Congress Cataloging-in-Publication Data

Rossman, Mark H., 1940–
Graduate school and beyond : earning and using your advanced degree / Mark H. Rossman.
p. cm.
Includes bibliographical references and index.
ISBN 978-1-59451-807-2 (hardcover : alk. paper)
ISBN 978-1-59451-808-9 (paperback : alk. paper)
1. Universities and colleges—United States—Graduate work. I. Title.
LB2371.4.R67 2010
378.1'55—dc22

2009050129

Printed and bound in the United States of America on acid-free paper that meets the standards of the American National Standard for Permanence of Paper for Printed Library Materials.

Designed and Typeset by Straight Creek Bookmakers.

14 13 12 11 10   1 2 3 4 5

To Jessica, Blake, Nicholas, Marlee, and Mia—
my grandchildren

CONTENTS

ACKNOWLEDGMENTS

A book of this type could not have been written had it not been for the experience I gained serving on more than 450 graduate committees at both on-campus and online universities since 1971. To my 80-plus master's graduates and 97-plus doctoral graduates: I have learned a great deal from each of you. Thanks to you all.

To my daughters, Kim and Nicole: You both have earned a PhD while being a wife and mother to our five grandchildren. I'm very proud of you.

I also want to particularly acknowledge the unwavering support of my wife, Dr. Maxine Rossman. She is a constant source of love, advice, and inspiration for everything I do. I'd be lost without her.

INTRODUCTION

The central theme of this book is that to succeed, graduate students need to be aware of the process of completing a graduate degree, control as many aspects of the process as possible, and be careful, skillful, and tactful negotiators. Simply stated, this book is designed to help students complete a graduate degree, regardless of how the degree is offered—online or on-campus.

I have worked exclusively with graduate students at the master's and doctoral level for more than forty years at both on-campus and online universities. I've served as a chair or major advisor for more than eighty master's degree graduates and more than one hundred doctoral graduates. In short, I know the graduate school process! In this book, I provide realistic answers to the questions and concerns most often raised by learners in graduate school. I describe the process of completing a graduate degree, identify relevant questions and concerns, and provide practical solutions and suggestions.

Chapter 1 addresses the uncertainties of many graduate school students. This chapter helps the reader to clarify reasons for being in graduate school, stresses the importance of time management, describes possible barriers to success, and identifies positive motivators. It ends with a discussion of the need for support at work and at home. Chapter 2 is devoted to earning a degree online. It stresses the place of online learning in degree programs and raises and answers a series of questions most often asked by learners new to this form of learning. Chapter 3 provides sources of information regarding financing a graduate degree. It also has a section on financial aid scams and how to avoid them. Chapter 4 provides useful information about developing and completing the program of study. Included is information on selecting the right degree program, understanding the program of study, and tips for taking online courses, time management, controlling frustrations, and keeping the mind, body, and spirit up while working on a graduate degree. Chapter 5 describes the roles and functions of the members of the graduate committee, as well as how to know and be known by potential committee members, and provides a guide to use when selecting committee members. Chapter 6 describes the comprehensive examination—the written comp and the oral comp—as well as how to prepare for it and how to successfully complete it. Chapter 7 is a discussion of the proposal and how it connects to the thesis or dissertation. The content of each chapter in the proposal and of the thesis or dissertation is discussed. Chapter 8 helps the reader to understand, prepare for, and successfully complete the defense of the thesis or dissertation. The book ends with Chapter 9, in which practical ideas are offered regarding what to do after completion of the degree. Included in this chapter are suggestions for binding, copyrighting, and publishing the final work, making up for lost time, developing a supplemental annotated transcript and portfolio resume, and making the degree work for you. The references include general style guides; guides for writing a proposal, thesis, dissertation, or research paper; researching and writing in the disciplines, and several useful Web sites for graduate students.

1

CAN I *REALLY* COMPLETE A GRADUATE DEGREE?

> When I completed my master's degree, I was sure I would never go back to school. Who would have believed it? Here I am working on my PhD.
>
> My biggest fear was that I could not do the work. My advice to others is to take one step at a time. Don't look up and don't look back. Just look to see what you have to do today. Know when to ask for help, and realize that this is part of the process.
>
> —*Pat*

Welcome to the world of graduate education. Reading this book is a good indication of your desire to earn a graduate degree. However, doing so won't be easy. You are in a world of the unknown—one that probably is just a little bit frightening. You are not alone. The *Digest of Education Statistics, 2002* reports that graduate enrollment in degree programs held steady at about 1.3 million in the late 1970s and early 1980s but rose about 34 percent between 1985 and 2000 (p. 201). Since then, graduate enrollment has continued to grow. In 2007 the Council of Graduate Schools indicated that 1,698,445 individuals were enrolled in graduate schools in the United States. Of that number, 902,977 (53 percent) were enrolled on a full-time basis and 924,229 (54 percent) of the total enrollment were women.

The numbers of graduate degrees awarded has also increased. In 1998 the council reported that slightly more than 446,000 individuals earned a master's degree and about 46,000 earned a doctorate. In 2005–2006 more than 594,000 individuals earned a master's degree and slightly more than 56,000 earned a doctorate. These numbers are expected to grow as well. *Projections of Educational Statistics to*

2017, a publication of the National Center for Education Statistics, predicts that between 2005–2006 and 2017–2018, the number of master's degrees awarded will increase 28 percent overall and the number of doctoral degrees will increase by 27 percent. Much of the increase will come from online degree granting institutions.

If you are completing your degree in an online, distance education, or e-learning setting you are in good company, because many of your colleagues are likewise enrolled in these rapidly growing programs. *Growing by Degrees: Online Education in the United States, 2008*—the sixth annual report of the Sloan Foundation on the state of online education in the United States—indicates that online education continues to be very much a part of mainstream higher education: 3.9 million students, or 20 percent of all higher education students, were taking at least one online course in fall 2007. This is a 12 percent increase over the number on online enrollments reported in 2006. A survey by the U.S. Department of Education's National Center for Education Statistics (NCES) found that in 2006–2007 enrollments in college-level, credit-granting online, hybrid/blended online, or other distance education courses at the graduate level were more than 2,349,000.

Over the years, I have spoken with many individuals who were thinking about entering graduate school. Some were quite ready whereas others have lingering doubts and questions about themselves. I don't know how many times I have heard: "Can I afford a graduate degree?" "How will working on the degree impact my family and job?" "Am I too old to be seeking a graduate degree?"

Can I Afford a Graduate Degree?

Let's begin by looking briefly at finances. This very important topic is also discussed later in this chapter (see Financial Support) and in more depth in Chapter 3.

Graduate school is not cheap. In 2009 average tuition, depending on location, program, and school, was around $31,000 per year. Online programs tend to be less expensive. Graduate students finance their degrees in a variety of ways including grants; scholarships; fellowships; work-study arrangements; teaching assistantships; home equity loans; employer tuition reimbursement; and borrowing from savings, parents, and commercial institutions.

The rare student who pays out of pocket for tuition and fees can take advantage of the Federal Lifetime Learning tax credit, which in 2009 was worth up to $2,000. The credit equaled 20 percent of the first $10,000 spent in tuition and fees each year. If you filed a single return, you were eligible for the full tax credit if your income was $45,000 or less and for a partial credit with income up to $55,000. For married couples filing jointly, the tax credit was fully available with income up to $90,000 and partially available up to $110,000. You could use the credit even if you didn't itemize deductions, and it reduced your tax bill dollar for dollar. As federal tax laws constantly change, be sure to check with a tax preparer for the most current information on this and other education-related tax credits, deductions, and advantages.

When considering if a graduate degree is worth the expense, keep this in mind: a 2007 report of the U.S. Census Bureau indicated that in 2006 holders of an academic doctoral degree earned an average of $61,091 per year and had an unemployment rate of 1.4 percent. Holders of the professional degree averaged $60,643 per year and had an unemployment rate of 1.1 percent. Master's degree holders earned an average yearly salary of $46,250 and had an unemployment rate of 1.7 percent. Bachelor's degree holders averaged $35,094 a year with an unemployment rate of 2.3 percent.

Earning a graduate degree pays for itself!

How Will Working on the Degree Impact My Family and Job?

There is no question that working on a graduate degree will impact your family and work routine. It is very difficult to find the time to complete all the requirements of a graduate degree without giving up something.

Before starting your degree program, it makes sense to be certain that your family not only supports your decision to return to school but also is aware of your need for time away from them. Don't assume that once you have made this decision, they support it. Discuss this fully with your spouse or significant other and, if you are a parent, your children. If the family includes older children, discuss how they can help out.

Consider going to school part-time, taking night classes, or signing up for online classes. Each option can save you time and money.

Many returning graduate students are working professionals. They have produced reports and conducted research related to their work situation. These are skills that will transfer to graduate school, where reports and research (i.e., class projects and papers) are prerequisites to success. When considering graduate school, think about the tasks performed at work and how these may relate to required courses. Many students fail to realize that they already have the basic research and reporting skills required for a graduate degree.

If appropriate, discuss your plans with your employer. Try to determine how your program will benefit you and your employer. Many adult-oriented degree programs stress practical application of knowledge. This means that class papers and projects may be directed to job-related problems. Don't make the often erroneous and outworn assumption that there is no connection between work and school. This may have been the case in years past, but for many of the more enlightened programs, this perception is passé.

Am I Too Old to Be Seeking a Graduate Degree?

Ah! Now I've let the cat out of the bag. Can you *really* do this at your age? Yes, you can! You do change with age, but barring major physical or mental deterioration you can still learn.

There are all sorts of studies to support the notion that adults are quite capable of learning new things well into their seventies and beyond. If you want to learn, you can. Age, in and of itself, will not prevent you from learning, though it can impact the learning process.

For example, it is not unusual for vision to start to decline in the mid-forties. The deterioration continues at a slow, gradual rate into one's seventies. Computer screens that once could be seen clearly about 12–18 inches away seemingly need to be pushed farther and farther away or pulled closer and closer in order to be seen clearly. The is a need for more light in order to read comfortably. Books may seem to be printed in smaller and smaller, blurry type. This is all part of the natural process of aging. In most cases, these problems can be attended to with eyeglasses and, in some cases, with surgery.

We live in a noisy world. Over time, noise can impact our ability to hear clearly. High frequency sounds and children's voices can become more difficult to hear. Rapid speech may be difficult to follow. You may even lose the ability to discriminate the sound of different letters. Did someone say "bad," or was it "dad"? Again, this is all part of the natural aging process and can be easily countered.

To top it all off, the aging process tends to slow down reaction time. Your reaction time may only be a nanosecond longer, but in that time a step has been lost or someone else, usually younger, gets in the first word.

The aging process can also create psychological problems that can influence learning, particularly if you are not aware of the natural process of aging. Excuses like "This wasn't the way it was in the good old days" or "Back when I was an undergrad, professors gave clearer lectures" often mask a decreasing self-confidence.

Experience is a two-edged sword that often interferes with learning. There is a classic scene in the 1986 movie *Back to School* where Rodney Dangerfield, as Thornton Mellon, a millionaire businessman, is in a lecture class in which the professor is extolling the theory behind "widgets" while Dangerfield refutes much of what is being said by using his own vast experience. This scene speaks to a common concern of many seeking a graduate degree—*I have more life experience than others in the class, including the professor!* Although you may indeed have a lot of life experiences and are used to doing things in a certain way, it may also be true that these experiences are getting in the way of learning new things.

Let's go back to the original question. Are you too old to earn a graduate degree? No, you are not. However, you need to be open to new experiences and recognize that things have changed and you are not the same person you were when you were an undergraduate. Pace yourself and plan your time so that you will not be overly stressed.

Before you get too involved with your studies, it is a good idea to get a complete physical examination. Be sure to have your vision and hearing checked and do whatever is necessary to help you overcome the natural process of aging. You can do it!

Remember that many learners who are seeking a graduate degree have some lingering doubts about their reasons for wanting a degree, their ability to complete a degree, their current scholastic abilities, and the impact that this process will have on their families, their jobs, or their way of life. Although we are not supposed to admit it, many of us are frightened of what lies ahead.

There is, however, much joy and excitement associated with completing a graduate degree. In addition to promotions, higher salaries, and new job responsibilities, the completion of this difficult objective is gratifying. A sense of personal accomplishment also accompanies the completion of a degree that, for many, has been a distant dream.

How This Book Can Help You

Many of the questions and concerns raised by both new and seasoned graduate students in traditional and distance education settings are identified in the present chapter. After completing this chapter, you should have a much better understanding of the concerns that face many individuals seeking a graduate degree. You will then be equipped to forge ahead with confidence and join countless others of all ages and from many different backgrounds who complete master's and doctoral degrees each year. They are doing it! So can you!

Chapter 2 discusses online courses and programs. It presents an overview of this rapidly growing, important, and relatively new way of delivering courses and degrees. In addition, it provides questions and answers that many learners thinking about online learning are concerned with.

Chapter 3 presents specific information about financing your graduate degree. It contains sources of funding at the federal, state, university, and college levels as well as information relative to paying for your graduate degree with loans from family and friends, savings and investments, and other private sources.

Chapter 4 describes how to develop and complete the graduate program of study, whether you are enrolled in a traditional "bricks-and-mortar" campus or a distance education program. The different types of graduate degree programs are discussed, along with selecting and developing courses that meet program requirements and personal goals; tips for success; understanding the relationship of the mind, body, and spirit, to the completion of a graduate program; controlling frustrations; and understanding the changing roles of family, friends, and others.

It is vital to understand the relationship of the graduate committee to success in graduate school. In Chapter 5 both the obvious and the subtle functions and roles of the committee are discussed. Techniques for becoming known by potential committee members and choosing an effective committee are also provided.

Chapter 6 discusses the comprehensive examination. The purposes and components of this exam are presented, and ways of preparing for it are explored. Several specific techniques for successfully completing both the oral and the written components of the exam are provided.

The completion of a thesis or dissertation is what essentially differentiates an undergraduate from a graduate program. This is the focus of Chapter 7. A well-designed proposal is critical to the development of the thesis or dissertation. This chapter helps the reader to understand and successfully use the proposal to guide the development of the thesis or dissertation and also presents tips and techniques about the parts of each chapter of the thesis or dissertation.

The defense of the thesis or dissertation is the focus of Chapter 8, which explains what is expected at a defense and provides several strategies for successful completion.

Chapter 9 contains information regarding what to do after the completion of the degree. Included is advice on how to use the time previously dedicated to program completion, binding the thesis or dissertation, copyrighting it, making it available for use by others, attending commencement, finding a job, publishing the thesis or dissertation, creating a supplemental annotated transcript, developing a portfolio resume, and other suggestions designed to take advantage of the newly earned graduate degree.

The book ends with references and a list of general style guides; guides to writing a proposal, thesis, dissertation, or research paper; guides to researching and writing in the disciplines, and useful Web sites for graduate students.

Why Am I in Graduate School?

If fifty graduate students seeking to earn a graduate degree were gathered together and asked to list one reason why they were in graduate school, a list with fifty different reasons probably would result. Many might speak of their desire to reach a personal goal, such as completing the degree for no reason other than that they want it. The need to comply with licensing requirements or other requisites for keeping or obtaining a job is also a motivation. Others may speak about the desire to learn something new or, simply, the desire to know. Still others may mention vague needs for personal fulfillment or the need to take part in a social activity, make new friends, or move on after experiencing a life transition.

All of the above are valid reasons for being in graduate school. However, it is important to remember that (1) if you want to teach at almost any level, you will need an advanced degree, (2) if you want to engage in research, an advanced degree will provide a distinct advantage over those with only a bachelor's degree, and (3) if you want to improve your skills or switch careers, an advanced degree will make you more marketable.

Three Categories of Learners

In 1961, Professor Cyril Houle published *The Inquiring Mind,* in which he reported on his seminal work that identified three basic categories of adult learners. Although dozens of similar studies have been conducted over the years, Houle's typology of adult learners remains a wonderful way to look at adult learners. Houle's three basic categories, used to describe individuals who participate in educational activities, are as follows:

- *Goal oriented*—those who are motivated to accomplish a specific goal or a clear-cut objective
- *Learning oriented*—those who are motivated to seek knowledge "for the sake of knowledge"
- *Activity oriented*—those who are motivated by the need for social interaction

It is not possible to always be placed in one category. However, one's dominant category depends on a number of factors such as what is being offered, when it is being offered, how much it costs, or the length of time the experience requires. Knowing something about the characteristics of the different types of learners is helpful when thinking about individual motivation and how this fits with graduate education.

Those who fall most frequently into the *goal-oriented* category are often impatient and believe that knowledge must be put to immediate use. They believe that pursuit of a purpose or objective is the primary motivation for obtaining a graduate degree. Learners in this category may experience difficulty with survey or introductory courses or those that are philosophical in nature because these courses tend to provide generalities or overviews, whereas the goal-oriented learner tends to want specifics.

Many professors in traditional graduate schools use the lecture format to deliver all their knowledge about a particular subject. They frequently ramble and go off on seemingly unrelated tangents. A goal-oriented learner may find this style difficult to cope with because this is not the preferred learning pattern of this type of learner.

The goal-oriented learner wants to see the immediate relevance of the information being presented and is frequently thinking, "So what! How does this affect me?" Regardless of a learner's dominant category, these seven words can help apply the information to a job or resolve a personal problem or concern. How does the experience relate to you today and tomorrow? How does it relate to your job, your home life, your self-development, or the world around you? Asking yourself these questions or asking them of friends, family, colleagues, or professors can help make the course's information or experience more personally meaningful.

The *learning-oriented* learner is one who seeks knowledge for the sake of knowledge. These individuals are usually avid readers who see education as a constant lifelong activity rather than occurring as episodic activities. This type of learner fits most closely with the philosophy of most graduate schools because their motivational patterns are most closely in tune with the ways in which graduate schools are organized.

This type of learner loves bibliographies and wants to know the genesis of each idea; all the various writers who have written on the subject; and all directly and indirectly related concepts, theories, constructs, or viewpoints. It is no wonder that this type of learner is a professor's dream.

The *activity-oriented* learner is frequently characterized as being gregarious, a "talker," or an extrovert. Individuals in this category are usually more outwardly than inwardly focused and seemingly want more to socialize with classmates rather than to acquire course content. This type of learner is seeking education more often to fulfill a social need than to acquire knowledge. Activity-oriented learners may view education as an escape. This type of learner also may find graduate school more difficult than anticipated because socialization is not the main purpose of any graduate program. This is particularly true in an online graduate program.

This is not to say that unless you are learning oriented you won't succeed in graduate school. It simply points out that the philosophy of most graduate schools more easily facilitates the learning-oriented learner.

Many people who have earned their master's or doctoral degree consider themselves very practical people who have clear-cut objectives, do not want to waste time on unnecessary activities, enjoy socializing, and don't see themselves as being particularly "learning oriented." Such individuals provide ample evidence of the two attributes that are absolutely necessary to complete anything in life: *drive* and *motivation.* With these attributes, almost anything is possible regardless of your dominant learning pattern. Without them, most things are more difficult.

The following activity is designed to help identify personal reasons for wanting a degree. To discover your own reasons, complete the following exercise.

Reasons for Wanting a Graduate Degree

Directions:

1. In the space immediately after the letters, list all the reasons you can think of for wanting a graduate degree. Be as specific as possible—that is, to be promoted to manager, to gain more information related to your interests in self-education, to be able to change careers, and so on. It might help to think of what you want to be doing 5 years from now in terms of professional and personal aspirations.

_____ a.
_____ b.
_____ c.
_____ d.
_____ e.

2. Go back to the reasons you listed for wanting a graduate degree and, in the blank before the letters, label each reason with either an E if it is Employment related or a P if it is Personal and not employment related.

Discussion: Many people have a variety of reasons for wanting to return to school. No one reason is better than another. However, it is important to think about and identify your reasons and motivation for desiring a graduate degree. Once you have completed this exercise, you should have a clearer idea of some of the real reasons why you want to complete your degree.

Motivation

How does motivation relate to success in graduate school? It is possible that you may be experiencing a little bit of doubt about your success or your degree program. How do you compare with your fellow learners? Why are you feeling concerned about being able to succeed when you know you have succeeded in a variety of other ways in the past? Are online or distance programs as good as traditional programs? Although the desire to earn a graduate degree is strong, concerns or fears about the unknown may be preventing you from achieving your goals. This is a classic *approach–avoidance* situation. Knowledge of what may be happening can provide the needed motivation to move forward. You will then be in a better position to take charge and control the situation rather than have it control you.

All people are motivated by drives. There are primary, innate drives such as hunger and thirst. And there are secondary drives such as desire, ambition, and fear. All drives are triggered by cues, which are little reminders that we have associated with our drives. Motivation is a result of having acquired a drive to attain a goal. The closer one gets to the goal, the more cues are present, and the greater is one's drive.

Cues can be negative or positive, depending on the situation. To give one example: a runner's drive increases closer to the finish line. The tape is in view, the crowd is roaring, the footsteps of other runners are heard in the background. The closer the runner gets to the finish line, the more powerful are the cues and the greater is the drive. But if the runner has on many occasions faltered at the point of victory, many of those same cues would become negative and serve as reminders of fear of past failures—the more similar this would be to the other races that had been lost and the greater would be the fear of failure.

Drives are triggered by cues. The same cue can thus be either negative or positive, depending on how it is perceived by the individual. You may want to achieve a graduate degree and have the drive to achieve, but you may also be avoiding it because fear of past failures, real or imagined, may be preventing you from starting or taking action to accomplish your goals. When the fear drive is stronger than the drive to achieve, action paralysis goes into effect, and movement toward earning the degree stops. The exercise on page 11 is designed to identify those cues that serve as positive motivators for you. Complete this exercise now.

Barriers to Learning

We are not as good at identifying those things that produce fear. What are some of the obstacles that may be preventing success?

K. Patricia Cross is a leading researcher on adult learning and the author of *Adults as Learners,* published in 1982. In her book, she discusses many of the barriers preventing learners from succeeding. Fears are imbedded in these barriers. Cross believes that most, if not all, barriers to learning can be grouped under one of three headings: situational barriers, institutional barriers, or dispositional barriers. She defines them as follows:

1. *Situational barriers* are those arising from one's situation in life at a given time. Examples are lack of funds, child care facilities, transportation, or support from one's family or employer.

My Positive Motivators

Directions: This activity is a two-part process. (a) In the spaces that follow, list all the reasons you can think of that relate to why you want to earn a graduate degree and list them in the appropriate column. Reasons can be personal (e.g., "I want it to complete my education" or "I will feel more complete as an educated person with the degree") or they can be professional (e.g., "I need it for my promotion" or "I will be a more viable consultant if I have it"). (b) Once you have completed Part 1, check with family, friends, and anyone else who knows you well enough to suggest additional motivators. Add them to the list.

Personal Motivators	*Professional Motivators*
1.	1.
2.	2.
3.	3.
Etc.	Etc.

Discussion: When this list is completed, it will serve as a visual reminder of the motivators encouraging you to complete your degree. Post the list in several conspicuous places. This could be on the bulletin board in your home work space, in your office, next to your computer, in your notebook, above your bed, on the refrigerator, or anywhere else you will constantly see it. The more visible the list, the more often it will be seen and serve as a motivator to help you complete your graduate degree.

2. *Institutional barriers* are those practices and procedures that exclude or discourage individuals from participating in educational activities. Examples are inconvenient schedules or locations, full-time fees for part-time study, majors that don't reflect one's interests, and professors who fail to understand the needs of their students.
3. *Dispositional barriers* are those related to attitudes and self-perception about oneself as a learner. Examples are that you feel you really don't like to read and study, you're not sure if online courses are as good as classroom-based courses, or you feel that you can't keep up with your fellow graduate students.

It is important to identify personally perceived barriers or obstacles that may prevent your success in graduate school. The following is an activity to assist with this assessment.

My Barriers to Learning

Directions: This activity is a two-part process. (a) Think about your life in terms of the situational, institutional, or dispositional barriers (or obstacles) that may be preventing your success in graduate school. Keep in mind that barriers are individually defined. What may be a barrier for one person may not be a barrier for another. List all the barriers you can think of in the spaces provided. You do not have to fill in all the spaces. (b) Discuss this list with your spouse, significant other, coworkers, or friends who know you well to see if they can help identify additional barriers, and add them to the list.

Situational Barriers (those arising from your current life situation that exclude you or discourage you from participating in graduate school):

1.
2.
3.
4.
5.
6.
7.
8.
9.
10.

Institutional Barriers (those practices and procedures you think are in place that exclude you or discourage you from participating in graduate school):

1.
2.
3.
4.
5.
6.
7.
8.
9.
10.

Dispositional Barriers (those personal attitudes and perceptions about yourself that you feel would prevent you from participating in graduate school):

1.
2.
3.
4.
5.
6.
7.
8.
9.
10.

Discussion: The purpose of this activity is to identify the fears and barriers that may be preventing you from getting started or making progress on your graduate degree. Simply identifying them is not enough. Action needs to be taken to eliminate them. Look at the source of the problem. Do you have the power to change or control it? How can it be modified? Many of the situational and dispositional barriers are ones that you can personally control because they frequently are problems related to an attitude you hold about yourself or your circumstances. You can choose to do things differently, such as not feeling guilty for changing the family routine while you are in graduate school. You have the power to eliminate barriers to success. Take action!

Time Management

To complete a graduate program, you need to be able to manage your time. It is very difficult to simply add the demands of a graduate degree to the many demands already placed on your time. It probably isn't possible to continue to do everything you have always done in addition to completing your degree. Something has to go in order for you to maintain your sanity and stay in control of your life. More than likely, you won't fully realize all that is required until the process begins. A usual reaction is to think "I have bitten off more than I can chew" or "I wish there were more hours in the day."

Good time management begins with a clarification and prioritization of personal objectives. To gain some control over your time, make time management a part of your everyday routine. How much time is needed and how much time can realistically be spent *every day* on such tasks as reading, thinking, writing, doing research at the library or online, and other similarly related degree tasks? Schedule time every day for these activities and keep to the schedule. Resist the temptation to take a long, hot bath during the time set aside to write or study.

Managing Course Time

Purposefully schedule time in your calendar for your schoolwork. If you are taking courses at the "U," this is not difficult, as classes are scheduled on a semester or quarter basis. If you are taking online courses, this becomes a bit more difficult, as you log in at your convenience. A bit of advice is to schedule your "log in" at the same time every week. Not scheduling time in your calendar increases the likelihood that you will not complete your course work.

Regardless of the course delivery format, when you are doing your course assignments it makes good sense to create an environment that says to you and your family, "I am doing course work, do not disturb." Some people set aside a part of their home as their classroom. When they are there, they are at school. Others wear specific clothing, such as a baseball cap, T-shirt, or sweatshirt, when they do course work. When they are wearing this clothing, they are not to be disturbed. This can work particularly well for students who have young children at home.

At the end of each day, pause and reflect on the things that were scheduled to be done. Were they done? Yes? No? Why not? How can today's errors not be repeated tomorrow? Only you can effectively plan your time, and only you can accept the blame or receive the credit concerning the accomplishment of daily objectives. Set realistic goals and plan your time wisely and effectively!

Time Wasters

One of the most useful things to do when trying to maintain control of your life is to think of things that waste time and then do something to get rid of the time wasters. The following is a list of the time wasters that apply to most graduate students:

1. Telephone interruptions
2. Friends or relatives dropping in uninvited when you are studying
3. Lack of clarity regarding learning objectives, priorities, and deadlines
4. Indecision and procrastination
5. Poor time management
6. Fatigue
7. Crisis management
8. Inability to say "no"

Take a good hard look at this list. How many of the time wasters apply to you? Do you let the telephone interrupt your working time? Why? Why not let it ring? Don't answer it; let the call go to voice mail or let the answering machine take it. If you don't have an answering device, get one. It is well worth the cost in terms of time management. This way you can complete the term paper during the time set aside for it rather than letting someone else control your time. How about Item 3 (lack of clarity regarding learning objectives, priorities, and deadlines)? How often have you set an objective and really stuck to the deadline you gave yourself to complete it? Item 8 (inability to say "no") is another problem for many people. Think about this: just because someone asks you to do something is not a reason for you to agree to it. Feel free to say "no," and don't feel guilty. Don't feel the need to give an explanation. You are completing your degree, and that is most important.

Self-Directed Learning

Self-directed learning is when individuals have primary responsibility for planning, implementing, and even evaluating the learning activity. Self-directed learning is an important operating principle of many graduate programs, and it is particularly important in distance education settings. Learners in graduate school must view themselves as active partners in the learning transaction and should try to control as much of the process as possible. They need to ask relevant and probing questions related to their own learning objectives. They need to view the teacher or professor as a resource for learning rather than as the sole conveyor of knowledge.

The Self-Directed Learning Self-Assessment Inventory on page 16 is helpful in predicting your success in a self-directed learning environment, a key feature of many graduate programs.

Becoming a Self-Directed Learner

There are several things you can do to become more proficient as a self-directed learner. The first is to think very clearly about your own learning needs. What do you want (or need) to learn? Practice the art of self-diagnosing your own learning needs. A key in this phase is also to consult with others who may be able to help you to clarify your learning needs. Next, set clear learning objectives related to your learning needs. Learning objectives should specify what you will learn, not what techniques or strategies you will use. Once you have translated your learning needs into learning objectives, you then need to specify the learning resources

Self-Directed Learning Self-Assessment Inventory

Directions: In the blank preceding each statement, use the following scale to rate the degree to which you feel you possess the listed requisites for self-directed learning. A discussion of the results follows the inventory.

1	2	3	4	5
NOT AT ALL		SOMEWHAT		COMPLETELY

____ 1. A concept of myself as being increasingly self-motivated

____ 2. An ability to relate to peers collaboratively

____ 3. An ability to see challenges as learning opportunities

____ 4. An ability to see peers as aids to my learning

____ 5. An ability to give help freely to others

____ 6. An ability to diagnose my own learning needs

____ 7. An ability to translate my learning needs into learning objectives

____ 8. An ability to see peers as resources for diagnosing needs

____ 9. An ability to seek out additional material and human resources as aids to my learning

____ 10. An ability to collect and validate evidence of accomplishment regarding my learning objectives

____ 11. An ability to relate to faculty as facilitators of my learning rather than as directors of my learning

____ 12. An understanding of my own learning style

____ 13. An ability to set my own standards

____ 14. An ability to adhere to my own standards

____ 15. An ability to manage my time effectively

Discussion: Total your score. If you have scored 50 or more, it is likely you will be able to succeed in a graduate school regardless of the delivery format—on campus or online. A score of less than 50 does not indicate that you will not succeed. It only suggests that you consider ways to improve your competency in those areas in which you scored 3 or less, as these are generally considered important factors in self-directed learning environments.

needed to accomplish your objectives. This is the section in which you list the material and human resources (books, articles, journals, and URLs to be read; people to be interviewed; manuals to be reviewed; etc.) you plan to use and the strategies you will employ to make use of them. What remains is to determine what you will produce as evidence of accomplishment of your learning objectives and a time line indicating when this material will be produced. What best provides evidence that you have accomplished your learning objectives? Will you produce a paper? Revise a syllabus? Write a manual? Produce a Web page?

Need for Support

Financial Support

Most graduate students pay for graduate school with some type of financial assistance. A 2006 publication of the National Center for Education Statistics indicated that during the 2003–2004 academic year, approximately 2.8 million students were enrolled in a graduate or first-professional program and that just under three-fourths (73 percent) of all graduate and first-professional students received some type of aid, including grants, loans, assistantships, or work study. The average amount of aid received by students was $15,100.

Most graduate students cannot pay for tuition, fees, books, and other school-related expenses by themselves and so rely on help from federal and state loans, the university, employers, family, friends, and other private sources. Those who do not receive some type of financial assistance at the graduate level are the exceptions to the rule. A fuller discussion of financing your graduate degree is presented in Chapter 3.

In addition to financial assistance, completion of a graduate degree requires the support of family, friends, coworkers, and employers. Support is also found in various social networking sites such as LinkedIn and Facebook.

Perhaps most important in this process is family. You need to fully discuss your plans, thoughts, fears, and hopes with them. Share as much as you can about your reasons for being in school. Help them to understand how important earning this degree is. Make sure all concerned know that there will be many changes in the time you can give to children or parents.

Many current lifestyle patterns will need to be changed for you to be successful. Like many people in graduate school, you are or will be working either as a research assistant or as a teaching assistant or will be gainfully employed off campus. It is common to be concerned about finding the time to go to class, read the assignments, prepare for tests, get online, and write term papers. You probably haven't even begun to think about all the time and effort required for the thesis or dissertation.

It is doubtful that you can continue to do all things at the same level of intensity at which you are now doing them. Something has to give. New ways will need to be found to complete responsibilities at work and at home. One way is to openly discuss concerns with those directly involved—that is, family, coworkers, and friends. Let's look at this more closely.

Family

At home, unless you are living alone, someone will have to either take over or take on a greater share of the household responsibilities. If this person is your mate, don't assume that he or she fully knows all that you do and knows what parts of your responsibilities you want to give up, share, or keep. This person is not a mind reader. Full and frank discussions will be needed.

If you really think about it, going to graduate school isn't easy for either of you. After all, your mate's lifestyle is changing as well. Perhaps he or she will need to spend more time with the children while you study. Perhaps he or she will need to assume more of the housekeeping chores such as doing the laundry, mowing the lawn, or changing the light bulbs. Everyone, including children, grandchildren, and parents, needs to have a clear understanding of what changes will take place and what this means to established routines. For example, it is common for family members to use the home computer for personal enjoyment. As your graduate work increases, you can anticipate that you will need more time on the computer. This potential conflict may be solved by purchasing a second computer and phone line more or less exclusively for your use.

If cleaning and cooking are your major responsibilities, discuss available options. Could your mate take over this task? Could someone come in once a week to clean the house? Are the children able to pitch in? Fast-food outlets are one way to relieve the cooking chores.

Open and honest communication is important. A frequent complaint of those with families who have returned to graduate school is that they really didn't know how many changes would be needed to complete their degree. They didn't realize the extent to which family routines would be disrupted. Realistically, weekends are not much fun for anyone when all you want to do is find time to study rather than go to a movie or to a restaurant. Children in a one-phone-line household can be more than a bit peeved when dad or mom is constantly online using the computer. Teenagers without access to the phone? Need I say more? No matter how much family support may be promised, when you are actually fully involved with working on your degree, it is often difficult for families to realistically deal with it.

There is no easy solution to this dilemma. A good suggestion is to continually discuss concerns and feelings. All involved need to make concessions at various times. Each person needs to give a little and know when to back off. It also helps when all are learning, progressing, and recognizing one another's accomplishments.

Try not to become so absorbed in your program that you trivialize or, worse, don't acknowledge the accomplishments of your mate or children.

Parents, siblings, and in-laws also need to be included when planning the successful completion of your graduate degree. To what extent are they able to help out? Don't assume that your parents are built-in baby-sitters.

It is not uncommon for extended families to get together on weekends and holidays. Thanksgiving dinner with one set of parents and Christmas dinner with the other set is a tradition in many families. Grandparents look forward to visiting with the grandchildren at these times. Although these visits are important in maintaining good, long-term family relationships, the weeklong annual get-together may not be possible while you are in graduate school. Phone calls to friends and family may need to be temporarily curtailed or shortened.

Many times, family members, particularly parents and in-laws, don't realize the extent of work that is involved in earning a graduate degree and feel left out when the visits stop or the phone calls aren't made as regularly as usual. Children resent time taken away from them so that you can go online. Let them know very early on that you are working to improve their future as well as your own and that the disruptions are only temporary. It is not easy to cut down on the things that are enjoyable or that bring joy to others.

Perhaps it will help to remember that the more time expended in completing the degree, the sooner it will be done and the sooner life can return to normal.

Most who have successfully completed a graduate degree would agree that it is very helpful to be in a supportive environment. This also implies a need to interact with individuals who know, understand, and accept the pressures you are under. Family, friends, and fellow students are very important in this regard. Often students form support/study groups to provide this support. This is discussed more fully in Chapter 6.

Work

Your work situation may need to change as the result of being in graduate school. The impact of graduate school on employment needs to be seriously considered. If you intend to remain employed while working on your degree and are worried about finding the time to do both and to do them well, openly and fully discuss this with your employer. Developing solutions before anticipated problems become serious provides for greater control of the situation. Consider the following: Will you be able to continue to work full-time? Can you work part-time? Is a four-day workweek an option? Can you use your computer at work to search for course-related material? Can you afford to quit your job and live off loans or teaching or research assistantships?

Perhaps you will not be able to fully anticipate the changes that will be needed at work. To more fully understand what is expected, talk with coworkers or others who have completed a graduate degree in situations similar to yours. This will help identify possible problems.

Once you have formed some idea of the changes that will be needed at work, discuss them fully with your employer as well. Perhaps a flextime arrangement in which you come to work early, stay late, or work at home or on weekends would provide the flexibility needed to attend classes during the day. Maybe you can eat lunch at your desk and use your computer to conduct online searches. Changing to a later work shift might also be a solution. Job sharing, a type of arrangement in which two people share one job, is another option. Remember, the worst that can happen is that the work situation cannot be changed. If this is so, and you need to earn money while in school, changing your current employment may be the only option.

Discuss with your employer the benefits of you receiving a graduate degree and how this can benefit both you and your employer. One idea in this regard is to try to develop final course projects that have direct application to your work situation.

Recently, a learner I know enrolled in a grants writing course as an elective in his MA in business graduate program. He wanted to learn more about how to secure and write grants that were appropriate to his professional interests. He discussed with his employer the time needed to develop the application and the obvious benefits to the company if the grant application was funded. The employer recognized how the company would benefit and allowed the learner to use a half day of company time each week to research and develop the grant application. All were thrilled when the application was submitted and ultimately funded!

Social Networks

One of the newest and more effective ways of providing and seeking support is through the use of social networks such as LinkedIn, Facebook, Twitter, and MySpace. Social networks are most helpful to graduate students as they usually consist of individuals who have similar interests, problems, and concerns. Early networks usually consisted of chat room discussions in which individuals discussed information, ideas, solutions, and so on regarding a variety of topics. There are several social networks specifically geared toward graduate students. These are discussed more fully in Chapter 6.

In addition to providing a venue in which graduate students can discuss common interests, social networks provide graduate students with the opportunity to form friendships that can transcend the graduate school process. They are also valuable for venting pent up emotions created through interactions between the learner, the committee, or the bureaucracy of the graduate school. It is not uncommon for learners to keep in touch well after they have completed their graduate degrees.

LinkedIn (www.linkedin.com) is an especially valuable social networking site when it comes to looking for a job once the degree has been completed. With more than 45 million users representing 150 industries around the world, LinkedIn allows members to create business contacts, search for jobs, and find potential clients. Individuals have the ability to create their own professional profile that can be viewed by others in their network, and also view the profiles of their own contacts.

There are literally hundreds of social networks available to you. Some are more useful than others. Prior to deciding which one(s) you choose to use and regardless of the security safeguards that may be in place, here are a few tips for practicing safe social networking:

1. Don't post personal information such as your Social Security number, student ID number, or home address and phone number. It is not difficult for a hacker to locate you, no matter how secure you think the site is.
2. Post only information that you are comfortable with others seeing. Many people can see your page, including professors, administrators, or prospective employers.
3. Once a post has been made, it can't be permanently deleted as it will exist on the pages of others in the group.
4. Be considerate of others and treat them as you would want to be treated. Although you should feel free to fully communicate with others in the group, remember that there are real people out there. A good rule might be to ask yourself if you would say it to their face.
5. Write out what you want to say before you post it to the group. This will give you the opportunity to check your spelling, context, and grammar. Even though no one will check it, you should always strive to make yourself look good.
6. Don't "flame" too much. Flaming is when an individual posts a strong opinion, statement, or message with no regard for holding back his/her emotions. Does this mean that you should never include emotional responses? Not at all. The release of pent-up emotions is a valuable feature of a social network. The key is to keep the emotions under control.

Supporters, Detractors, and In-Betweeners

> *Supporters:* Those who support your graduate school plans.
> *Detractors:* Those who are against your graduate school plans.
> *In-Betweeners:* Those whose words or actions make it difficult to know if they are for or against your graduate school plans.

As related to success in graduate school, the comments and actions of most family, friends, employers, and colleagues can generally be categorized by the ways in which they either help or hinder your progress. Individuals who are in favor of what you are doing are supporters. Those who are against you are detractors. Sometimes it is difficult to determine if a person is a supporter or a detractor. These are in-betweeners.

Supporters. Supporters may be friends, colleagues, or family members who provide constructive criticism or who challenge you to strive for greater accomplishments. They show support through words of encouragement, sensitivity to the need for study time, or action to take over household chores that you have done in the past. These individuals may also be faculty members, mentors, or other role models who provide sage advice as well as assistance.

Detractors. Some people do not want you to succeed. They may be envious or jealous of you. Whatever their reasons, they drain your energy and can make life difficult.

They may be ambitious fellow students who take every opportunity to belittle you and other graduate students. Their techniques can be subtle, but they frequently seek to build themselves up in the eyes of the professor by devaluing your contributions in class and in the online discussion forum or by capitalizing on incorrect responses to questions posed by the professor. Rather than trying to understand them, the best advice is to avoid them.

In-Betweeners. Some people, especially family, like you just the way you are and do not really look forward to the changes that will occur after graduation. They may be just a bit apprehensive about your future plans, or they may simply not adapt well to change. Their words or actions convey neither support nor opposition.

It is common for in-betweeners to not volunteer an opinion or to not express it when asked. Frequently they don't want to offer their opinion because it might seem to be contrary to the new direction in your life, or they may not want to express a counter opinion because they want to avoid a possible confrontation. When a decision has been made, they are fairly passive and do what they have to with little or no enthusiasm. It is difficult to determine any hidden meanings from their words or actions.

It might be useful to think about how to deal with each type of person, as this will help ensure that maximum benefit will be obtained from supporters, and that the negative force of the detractors and in-betweeners will be neutralized.

Going to graduate school demands much of you and those around you. It will not be easy, and it will not be more of the same in terms of undergraduate work. It is a challenging prospect, especially if it has been a while since you were last in school. However, keep in mind that things have changed. You have changed. By carefully looking at the reasons you want a graduate degree and taking care to rearrange your life to be able to take on this new responsibility, you will be able to make it. Don't be afraid. Go for it!

2

ONLINE COURSES AND DEGREES

> When I was taking my undergraduate degree, the only way I could complete my course work was to attend classes on campus. It was OK then as I didn't have a job and family responsibilities as I do now. Today, I am in grad school. If I couldn't take online courses, I don't know how I would complete my degree.
>
> —*Illile*

The way colleges and universities deliver courses today is much different from the way it was in the past. No longer does going to class mean being physically in the classroom. Attending a class on campus once a week for three hours is a thing of the past for many of today's graduate students. Enrolling in online, distance, or e-learning classes is a viable option to enrolling in on-campus classes. Online learning, distance education, and, more recently, e-learning all refer to the acquisition of knowledge and skill using electronic technologies such as computer- and Internet-based courseware and local and wide area networks. For the remainder of this chapter, "online" will be used to refer to electronically mediated, Web-based courses and degrees.

As mentioned in Chapter 1, almost 4 million students took at least one online class in 2007. It should come as no surprise that traditional brick-and-mortar students use the Internet to secure information relative to their on-campus classes. Many professors assign material that requires the use of the computer to research ideas, opinions, and sources to validate what is written in a class paper or project, or to access online libraries. This is quite common and frequently required in many on campus courses.

In July 2009, about 65 million people visited Wikipedia (http://en.wikipedia.org/wiki/Main_Page), a Web-based free source of information containing millions of articles in more than 270 languages. Many professors don't encourage students to use Wikipedia as the articles are not "peer reviewed" and contributors need no special training or education to contribute an article. However, this form of online education as well as the hundreds of social networking sites—Facebook, MySpace, LinkedIn, and Twitter being among the most popular—is heavily used. So even if you don't plan to take an online course, it is important to be aware of this form of online learning and to know how it relates to earning your graduate degree.

This chapter discusses the online learning phenomenon, its background, advantages, and disadvantages, and answers frequently asked questions about online course and programs. It ends with a self-assessment designed to help determine if this option is for you. If you have an interest or want to know more, read on. If not, you might skip to Chapter 3.

Development of Distance (or Online) Education

When online education courses were initially introduced, many institutions thought of this new way to deliver courses and degrees as simply a way to deliver material electronically. Many early efforts were little more than correspondence courses delivered over the Internet. As interest and research grew in the new delivery system, refinements were made. Though somewhat better, these newer versions were little more than "talking heads" delivering lectures to individuals in distant settings. These early attempts provided for little discussion or personal interaction with the material. As a result, early attempts at online courses were viewed by many as less desirable than on-campus courses. Plus, the preparation of such courses demanded more time from the professors delivering the course—a commodity many professors did not have. As a result, the effectiveness of early attempts at online learning was questionable.

As research and experience established what was needed to make online courses more effective, course developers (individuals with knowledge of how to effectively develop computer-based courses) were frequently teamed with professors who had content knowledge but lacked online course development skill. Creating teams with process and content knowledge led to more and more effective use of online courses.

A great deal of research today speaks to the value of online learning. There are advantages and there are disadvantages. The research also raises important questions for those who have never taken an online course. Let's take a closer look.

What Are the Different Types of Online Courses?

Online courses usually take one of three forms: enhanced courses, hybrid (or blended) courses, or fully online courses.

Enhanced courses are essentially on-campus courses that use technology to enhance the course. The online components may be links to various supplemental materials, class notes, the class syllabus, or an online lounge or discussion group.

Hybrid (or blended) courses combine on-campus classroom attendance with online technology. Blended courses can reduce on-campus time by utilizing a discussion board to facilitate discussion on a topic rather than requiring students to be physically in class. Other traditional course requirements such as tests, readings, or tutorials can be completed via the Internet.

Fully online courses are offered entirely over the Internet and do not require students to physically be on campus. Fully online courses may be *asynchronous* or *synchronous.* In an asynchronous online course, unit or weekly requirements are most often available at the beginning of the course. The professor usually posts discussion questions relating to the unit assignment(s). Students post responses to these questions as well as responding to the posts of others in the class, including the professor. Communication is achieved through the classroom discussion board as well as through e-mail, voice mail, and fax. Discussion boards usually use threaded discussions that allow all class participants to see and review everything that has been posted. Synchronous online courses use real-time communication as the primary means of communication and interaction. This means that all class participants must be online at the same time.

Why Should I Enroll in an Online Course?

Online courses usually have no scheduled times when you must be "in class"—which is to say, at your computer. Thus, you can plan your own schedule regarding when you will enter the "classroom," complete assignments, and post responses. No one knows (and no one cares) if you are in your pajamas and it's three o'clock in the morning.

You won't have to stand in line to enroll for class. If you are enrolled in two or more courses, you won't need to be concerned about traveling from one classroom to another or from opposite ends of the campus to get to class. Most online classes provide for online enrollment. Once you are online, it is easy to go from one class to another.

From a financial perspective, you will save money by taking online courses. You do not have to commute or pay for parking, and you won't need to give up your job and attend campus as a full-time student. However, although the PhD requirement of one year in residence as a full-time student is becoming less and less of a concern at many colleges and universities, it still is a requirement at some. If you are a parent, the flexibility of online courses usually works well with parental responsibilities as well as saving on child care expenses.

What Are Some Differences Between Online and On-Campus Classes?

A major difference between online and on-campus classes relates to the amount and quality of discussions. Students in online classes usually provide more thoughtful and in-depth responses than those in face-to-face classes as they have had more time to read the assignment and think about what they want to say. This is very different from on-campus classes, in which the professor asks a question and expects an immediate response. Adults usually respond better when they have time to relate the question not only to the reading or the lecture but also to their own experience. This greater flexibility frequently produces greater student satisfaction, confidence, and overall performance.

The flexibility of online courses has enabled universities to expand their boundaries far beyond the physical confines of the campus. Classes are no longer restricted to those who can attend regularly scheduled classes on campus. As a result, enrollment in online classes tends to be geographically quite diverse and reflect the thoughts and opinions of individuals from many miles away. It is not unusual for online classes to have participants from many different states and countries. This diversity brings a very rich perspective to class discussions.

Students in online classes tend to earn better grades than their on-campus counterparts. This may well be due to being able to think before responding.

The use of technology is a major component in online courses. The need to be "computer-savvy" is a concern to many potential online learners, particularly older adults who are not comfortable with the computer. Most colleges and universities offering online courses provide tutorials or information about computer requirements needed to successfully complete their online courses. Some universities even offer free pre-enrollment seminars using the same course delivery format used in all online courses to provide answers to the computer hardware and software and Internet connections needed.

What Are Some Strategies to Help Me Complete an Online Degree?

Success in an online environment is not very different from success in the on-campus environment. In both situations, success comes when you are able to manage both your relationship with your college or university and your course work. When managing your relationship with the university, you need to take responsibility for your own education. Determine what you want from your degree; then discuss this with course facilitators, advisors, and faculty. Don't be passive and expect the institution to do this for you. Depend on yourself and take responsibility for your own learning.

There are several strategies for managing your course work:

- Make two or three weekly appointments with yourself to complete course work. The first one, preferably early in the week, should be used to complete any course readings or assignments; then to respond to the discussion questions or other assignments. The others should be to respond to learner postings or to provide additional questions or comments. Try to keep the same appointment times each week as this will help create a habit. As you know, habits are hard to break.
- Create a specific space or wear specific clothing when you are working on your courses. This is like the "do not disturb" button on the phone. When you are in this place or wearing your schoolwork clothing, friends, family, and coworkers will recognize that you are working on course work and are less likely to interrupt you.
- Get to know your course facilitator as well as possible. In an online environment, you can't stop into the office but you can make contact via e-mail, phone, and fax. Make sure the contact is course-related and not viewed as brown nosing or a waste of the professor's time. For example, you could send the professor an e-mail with new supplemental course-related information or a new site found on the Web. Check to see if he or she maintains online office hours, and don't hesitate to use this time for course-related questions. More information on getting to know your faculty is presented in Chapter 5.
- Determine if your university provides formal or informal discussion groups not connected to the course. Many universities offer these types of online discussion groups to help students support one another, to raise course-related questions that may seem too trivial to mention in class, and to maintain motivation.
- You can also save the responses that were posted in the discussion forum. This is a particularly good idea, as you will have another resource when studying for the exam or preparing for comps.

How Do I Complete and Hand in Assignments?

As in on-campus courses, assignments—including required reading, locating additional Web sites, and unit discussion questions—are usually completely presented in the course syllabus. You can view and print out this material at your leisure. You complete assignments just as you would in an on-campus class; then submit them to the professor via e-mail attachments, post them in the discussion room, or follow the instructions in the syllabus.

What Is the Average Age of Online Class Participants?

This is difficult to answer, as it will vary with the class and the institution. As a general rule, online graduate learners are older than their on-campus counterparts. It is important to remember that age isn't a barrier to learning to well into one's seventies. Even at this age, there is nothing to suggest that the ability to learn stops. If you did well as an undergraduate, you will probably do well as a graduate student. The biggest difference is that as you age, you will likely need more time to complete assignments than you did as an undergrad.

How Are Online Courses Graded?

In online courses, course requirements and grading criteria are usually included in the syllabus. These may include checklists and rubrics. A checklist is an objective evaluation to determine whether the criteria have been met. For example, if participation is part of the evaluation criteria, a course checklist will probably have an item that records whether you did or did not participate. The course facilitator is usually responsible for making this determination and simply looks at your participation in the course discussion room and makes that determination. The use of rubrics is another way of grading. A rubric provides descriptions of different levels of expected performance. The instructor evaluates the level of participation and enters a grade using the grading rubric.

Many online classes provide a place in the course for you to see the instructor's assessments and/or grades. If participation in each weekly unit is assessed and recorded on a regular basis, you will have a good understanding of what is expected and the degree to which you are meeting these expectations. This common form of online grading also provides an ongoing way for you to anticipate your final grade.

The use of checklists and rubrics are usually applied to all course requirements, including the final project or paper. Though there is no set rule, more often than not the final paper or project and class participation are important parts of the final grade. It is important for you to know and fully understand how the checklists and/or rubrics are applied and what options, if any, you have if your perceptions of the degree to which you are meeting the criteria differ from that of the instructor.

Quizzes and tests can also be delivered via the computer. This is a relatively simple procedure and one that you have probably already used. You may have participated in an online survey asking you to rate the particular service you received after taking your car in for service. You are directed to a particular site, and a series of questions with spaces for your answers is provided. This is the same format used for giving tests or quizzes in many online classes. Keep in mind that in online classes, especially at the graduate level, tests and quizzes frequently take on less importance as more reliance is placed on participation, application, and final papers.

A frequent concern raised about online classes that can also be leveled at on-campus classes relates to determining that the person submitting the paper or completing the test is actually the person enrolled in the class. It is not uncommon for some colleges or universities to ask you to come to a testing center and take the test in person or with a proctor. Also, there are many commercial sources that are designed to detect plagiarism or other forms of cheating (e.g., plagiarismdetect.com, copyscape.com, mydropbox.com, and turnitin.com).

How Much Time Will It Take to Complete Online Courses and the Degree?

This is another one of the hard-to-answer questions, as it depends on your learning style and the nature of the course or degree.

Online courses will require anywhere from 6–20 hours per week, depending on the nature of the course, your experience, learning style, knowledge, computer expertise, and typing ability. Generally your first online course will be the most frustrating as you are learning not only course content but also the course delivery platform. For example, learning how to post responses to the unit discussion questions takes practice, but once you know how to do it, you don't have to learn it again for the next course. Expect to spend more time at the end of most courses completing papers and other assignments.

The time required to complete an online degree also varies depending on the nature and type of degree (master's or doctoral) and the number of courses that you can complete in a term. It is not uncommon for master's degrees to be completed within 12–18 months and doctoral degrees to be completed in 3–4 years. I have worked with several online learners who have taken as long as seven years to earn their doctorate.

Generally, it is recommended to take fewer courses in the first term than you might take in later terms. This will remove some of the pressure relating to learning both course process and content.

Life often waylays well-designed plans. Juggling the demands of family, job, and school is difficult. It is made even harder by a demanding boss, a sick child, or an elderly parent. These concerns are the same whether you are in an online or an on-campus program. The best advice is to plan for the unexpected. Expect that you will not be able to control all the time variables. This is especially true when completing your thesis or dissertation.

What Technology Is Needed to Participate in an Online Course or Degree Program?

You do not need to be technology-savvy to take an online course or enroll in an online graduate program. Most colleges and universities list the minimum computer configuration and skill requirements needed to participate in their courses or degree programs.

You will need a computer that is in good working order. It may be either a laptop or a desk top. You should be comfortable with your computer and know how to get it fixed if it breaks.

You should also have Internet connectivity through either a modem or broadband connection and be able to easily connect to the Web. The ability to send and receive e-mail and upload and download files is also important. A printer is strongly suggested, as some learners find it difficult to read material on a computer and prefer to print it out.

Many reputable online programs provide free trial visits in which you will actually experience what it feels like to participate in an online class. This is a great service that will reduce your fears while providing practical, hands-on experience.

How Effective Are Online Courses?

When online classes began, effectiveness was frequently brought into question by university personnel who had little other than their opinions and limited experience to support their feelings that online could never be as effective as on-campus courses. As is the case with many educational innovations, there were proponents on both sides of the issue. Traditionalists, particularly at the graduate level, argued that graduate education could only be effective on campus. After all, this is the way it had always been done. Online learning proponents argued that there was little other than opinion to back this claim and sought to provide research to indicate that quality education could be delivered online. One of those in the latter category who raised this question and sought to provide an answer was Dr. Thomas L. Russell. The fifth edition of his highly influential book, *The No Significant Difference Phenomena: A Comparative Research Annotated Bibliography on Technology for Distance Education,* as well as the companion Web site, www.nosignificantdifference.wcet.info/index.asp, has reviewed more than 355 media comparison studies (MCS) from as far back as 1928. Alternative delivery systems such as correspondence study, radio, television, and online have been reviewed. Russell's overwhelming conclusion is that when course materials and teaching methodology are constant, there are no significant differences between student outcomes in distance learning courses compared to face-to-face courses.

In 2009 the U.S. Department of Education published *Evaluation of Evidence-Based Practices in Online Learning: A Meta-Analysis and Review of Online Learning Studies.* This report identified and analyzed more than 1,000 empirical studies of online learning published from 1996 through July 2008. It concluded that "classes with online learning (whether taught completely online or blended) on average produce stronger student learning outcomes than do classes with solely face-to-face instruction" (p. 18).

Another very good way of determining online effectiveness is to speak with individuals who are involved with online courses: students, professors, and administrators. With so many people taking online courses, it should not be difficult to locate and talk with students in online programs. Speak with as many current and former students as possible. Speak with faculty and administrators. Try to determine if certain trends or patterns emerge. Listen carefully for bias and negativity. Remember that if you hear of a bad or negative experience, it is important to know why it was bad. Remember that the negative experience is only the experience of one person. Simply to accept this person's negative experience without digging more deeply into the circumstances is to give away your freedom of choice.

What Skills Are Needed to Succeed in Online Courses?

Many of the skills for success you learned in on-campus classes are also needed in online classes. You will need to complete weekly assignments on time, submit research papers, and participate in class discussions. The major difference between these two delivery methods is that in online courses you will not do this in real time.

One of the most important skills you will need is to be able to manage your time. It is very difficult, if not impossible, to take on the considerable demands of a graduate program without carefully considering the time needed for class work. Where will this time come from? What activities will you give up or postpone? When will you go online? Mornings? After work? After the kids are asleep? Effective time management is crucial.

Life management is another critical skill. You need to skillfully balance the demands of job and family and still maintain time for social activities, spiritual development, and leisure.

Asking complete and relevant questions is a skill that is especially important in online classes. In this environment, questions and responses are usually preserved in the form of a threaded discussion. This means that everyone in the class can read and respond at their leisure. Class members have the opportunity to think about what they will write. Professors are aware of this and often expect fuller and richer responses than they might in an on-campus class. Feel free to ask relevant questions of the instructor and your classmates. However, be courteous and tactful when raising questions and responding to other class participants.

Good writing skills are needed in online classes. Though many online classes incorporate nonwritten material, such as streaming video and recorded lectures, the majority of online classes depend on the written word. In online classes, most of the class discussion is in the form of threaded discussions. Good writing skills are essential to fully respond to unit questions as well as to respond to the postings of fellow classmates. Written responses should be clear and succinct. They should flow logically and be easily read. Each sentence should reflect proper grammar, spelling, and syntax.

Do Online Learners Feel Isolated?

Contrary to what you might think, most learners in most online education programs do not feel isolated from each other. Quality programs use many means to develop a strong sense of community. In well-designed online programs, learners often find faculty to be more accessible than in traditional classrooms, as online support groups, learner chat rooms and forums, online help desks, and online bookstores continually support and connect learners. Many degree programs incorporate online student lounges as part of their socializing efforts. University-sponsored Twitter, Facebook, MySpace, and other social networking spaces are frequently used to build and foster online communities.

If anything, online learning can be more challenging because it puts more responsibility on the learner. In a classroom-based course, having to show up for class is a motivator. It's up to e-learners, in contrast, to pace themselves and follow through the course. This type of course work usually works best for the motivated learner who is ready to share the responsibility for learning with teachers or classmates.

Is "Online" Right for You?

Whether an online graduate degree plan will work for you depends on many variables, including your preferred learning style, your time management skills, the philosophy of the university, and your goals and desires. Re-read the questions and answers posed in this chapter and think about how this information applies to you.

To further help you with this question, you might want to complete the following self-assessment.

Is "Online" Right for Me?

Directions: Read each of the ten items. In the space below each item, place a check mark in the answer that most closely represents your response. Once you have completed all ten items, read the interpretation that follows.

1. Do you have regular access to a computer with an Internet connection?

   ____ yes ____ no

2. Do you know how to use e-mail and word processing software?

   ____ yes ____ no

3. Are you self-motivated and self-disciplined?

   ____ yes ____ no

4. Do you have good reading and writing skills?

   ____ yes ____ no

5. Do your family and friends support your decision to take an online course?

   ____ yes ____ no

6. Do you possess strong time management skills?

   ____ yes ____ no

7. Do you enjoy working independently?

   ____ yes ____ no

8. Do you enjoy a challenge?

   ____ yes ____ no

9. Are you able to commit ample time (about 8–20 hours) each week to your online course(s)?

   ____ yes ____ no

10. Are you comfortable participating in Facebook, MySpace, and other social networking or discussion groups?

    ____ yes ____ no

Interpretation: If you answered "yes" to six or more items, online learning is a good option for you. If you answered "yes" to 3–5 items, online learning is a possibility. If you answered "yes" to fewer than three items, online learning is probably not a good option.

There are many points to consider when making a decision about participating in online learning; only you and you alone can make the final decision.

3

FINANCING YOUR GRADUATE DEGREE

> I couldn't believe how expensive it was to go to graduate school. I had saved some money but didn't have all that I needed to cover tuition, books, and all the other costs associated with earning my PhD. I didn't know what to do. I couldn't give up my job as I needed to support my family. Luckily, I spoke with the human resource director at my company and the financial aid officer at my local university. I was given tips that helped finance my degree. Without financial aid, I would not have been able to earn my degree.
>
> —*Andrew*

Relatively few graduate students finance their program without some type of financial assistance. Most pay for their education through a variety of sources such as various federal and state loans, assistantships, grants, gifts and/or loans from the university or college, tuition reimbursement programs from employers, personal savings or investments, gifts or loans from parents and family, or other sources, such as private foundations (of which there are hundreds) or philanthropic organizations. When seeking any type of financial assistance, it is essential to determine if the material you are reading, including the information is this book, is up-to-date.

Federal Sources

Several federal grant and loan programs are available for graduate students. These programs are constantly changing, so it is very important that you understand the most current application procedures and instructions. Usually, these programs require that the recipient meets need criteria, is working toward a degree or certificate in an eligible program, is a U.S. citizen or eligible noncitizen, and is making satisfactory academic progress.

Perhaps the most comprehensive source of federal money for graduate students is available through the U.S. Department of Education's Federal Student Aid Information Center (800-433-3243, http://studentaid.ed.gov/PORTALSWebApp/students/english/index.jsp). Ask for a complete description of all programs that may be of interest to you. If you contact the center by e-mail, be sure to include as much information as possible about your degree program, interests, and needs, as this makes the response easier and more meaningful. When you apply for federal loans you need to complete the Free Application for Federal Student Aid (FAFSA), which is available at www.fafsa.ed.gov/.

When considering loans, realize that most of them need to be paid back shortly after graduation or when you are no longer enrolled in a degree program. Learners enrolled in graduate programs can borrow, usually at competitive interest rates, from the following federal sources:

Carl D. Perkins Loan Program: provides up to $6,000 per year for graduate studies with a cap of $40,000.

Stafford Student Loan (SSL) Program: fixed-rate student loans for graduate students attending college or university at least half-time. There are two types of Stafford loans—subsidized (awarded based on financial need) and unsubsidized (awarded with no regard to financial need). A lifetime limit of $138,500 with various conditions may be borrowed from this source.

Grad PLUS loan: fixed-rate, non-need, credit-based loans guaranteed by the federal government. The yearly limit is equal to the cost of attendance minus any other financial aid received.

Federal Direct Loan Program: provides up to $20,500 per school year for graduate students.

Much more information about federal loans for graduate school is available at http://studentaid.ed.gov/PORTALSWebApp/students/english/gradstudent.jsp.

Although most federal programs providing grants or loans are directed at students enrolled in campus-based programs, many are applicable to distance-learning students as well. For example, in certain situations, a Pell Grant may be available to a person studying at a distance.

Don't assume that having been denied a loan as an undergraduate, you will be denied again as a graduate student. At the graduate level, financial aid is based on a different set of criteria. Because there is much detailed paperwork regarding federal financial aid, it is essential to work closely with the financial aid office regarding the timetables, forms to be completed, and other regulations affecting the loan process.

Military personnel also have unique options for federal assistance. Because the amount and type of assistance varies, it is best to check with a local Veterans Administration office for specific details. Active-duty military personnel, including members of the National Guard and Armed Forces Reserve, have at least two options available: (1) in-service benefits through the U.S. Department of Veteran Affairs, and (2) tuition assistance from the military person's respective service administered by the Defense Activity for Non-Traditional Educational Support (DANTES; http://www.dantes.doded.mil/Dantes_web/counselorsupport/scholaships.asp). The Military Educational Service Officer can provide more information for eligible students.

In addition to the federal assistance plans, some states also have educational benefits available for veterans and military personnel. Questions about these possibilities should be directed to the state veterans or military affairs offices. A list of the state directors of Veterans Affairs is available at www.nasdva.net/. Information regarding the Montgomery GI Bill and other military educational benefits is available at www.gibill.va.gov.

Also, be sure to check the most recent edition of the Catalog of Federal Domestic Assistance (CFDA), at www.cfda.gov/index. Although it takes some effort to master this very complete list of all federal domestic assistance programs, it is well worth the time.

State Sources

Financial assistance is available from a variety of state sources as well. Usually, the student needs to be a resident of the state to receive state funds. As individual state requirements vary, it is advisable to contact the financial aid staff in your state department of education and ask about loans or grants available to graduate students. Many state departments of education maintain a library that contains a variety of aid sources. If possible, make a trip to the state department of education and meet with the financial aid person. While there, be sure to look for any other state, federal, private, or public sources that may provide assistance. A list of addresses, phone numbers, and e-mail addresses for state higher education agencies can be obtained at http://wdcrobcolp01.ed.gov/Programs/EROD/org_list.cfm?category_cd=SHE.

University or College Sources

When it comes to financing education, the most knowledgeable person is the college or university financial aid officer. Get to know him or her soon because this person is aware of a variety of sources of funding specific to your university and can provide good advice regarding current federal loan programs and other possible sources of money, such as scholarships or grants from state, college, or university sources.

However, don't rely totally on financial aid personnel, because there are several sources, such as grants from foundations with specific purposes, of which the financial aid officer may not be aware. For example, if your heritage is Polish, you may apply for a grant from the Kosciuszko Foundation in New York City. In 2007 this foundation awarded $1.1 million to finance domestic scholarships for 114 Polish Americans involved with Polish studies, and it funded a U.S.-Polish exchange program. The foundation's programs and opportunities are for Americans to study language or conduct research in Poland and for Poles to conduct research or to teach in the United States.

Another common source of financial assistance for graduate students is through a teaching assistantship (TA) or a research assistantship (RA). Basically, a TA requires the recipient to teach in return for money and/or benefits such as reduced tuition or medical coverage. RAs are more nebulous but generally require the recipient to engage in research, usually on a professor's research project.

An intangible benefit of both types of assistantships is that recipients become known by the professors and get to know the professors as well. This is helpful when selecting committee members. This topic will be discussed in more detail in Chapter 5.

Be sure to personally check with the department or college for departmental grants and teaching and/or research assistantships, because these programs may not be as well known to the financial aid office as they are within your graduate department.

Employers

Many employers have tuition assistance programs (TAPS) or other company funds available to pay college costs. The National Center for Educational Statistics noted that in 2003–2004, 27.9 percent of master's students and 22.7 percent of doctoral students received employer assistance to help finance graduate education. Employers frequently provide funds for graduate students because the company generally recognizes the ultimate benefit not only to you but also to the company. It is a common practice today for companies and universities to work together to provide individualized on-site degree programs. Many companies offer scholarships, tuition reduction or reimbursement plans, or distance training opportunities with their partner universities. This type of financial assistance at the graduate level may be qualified, which means that it may be tax-free. Check with your human resources office for current information. Because many of these programs are private and vary in terms of how much funding is available, repayment terms, and other qualifications, you are well advised to speak with your employer's human resource office to learn if your company has funds of this nature and if they are available to you. Even if the company does not provide such a program, it might make sense to request financial assistance from your employer, stressing the advantages to both you and the company. The worst that can happen is that the company will say "no."

Family

Parents and family are another good source of financial assistance. Often, it is easier to get a loan or a gift of money from parents or family than from any other source. It makes good sense to treat this source of funds as you would any other. This means fully discussing your needs, the amount needed, and repayment terms. Recognize, too, that just because funds are needed to finance your degree, this may not be a sufficient reason for family to provide it.

Younger graduate students may not realize that as parents age, they often feel a greater need to provide for their own future, and even though they have the best of intentions, they may not be able or willing to provide additional funds for your graduate degree.

Savings and Investments

Many individuals feel the best way to finance an education is to use savings or investment funds. Although this may seem to make sense, some financial advisors insist that it makes more sense to borrow at the usually lower rates for educational loans than to deplete savings accounts or liquidate investments and lose the interest on these accounts. If you are considering withdrawing funds from savings or selling investments to finance your graduate education, consult with a financial advisor regarding the best way to secure the necessary funds.

Additional Sources

A particularly good source for exploring private funding is a free computerized service from FastWeb. You complete a questionnaire, submit it, and receive an e-mail containing a customized list of financial aid sources. To use this service, log on to www.fastweb.com.

Finding the many sources of aid that might be available to you can seem a daunting task. But just like anything else, the more you are aware of potential sources of assistance, the more you control the process. The most effective way to find information on how to finance your education is through the Web or through online national data bases.

The following is a list of selected financial aid sources that will provide additional information on financing your education:

- *Fellowships and Grants,* American Council of Learned Societies, www.acls.org/grants/default.aspx?id=354.
- *Grant Programs,* National Endowment for the Humanities, www.neh.gov/grants/index.html.
- *Fulbright: Fellowships for U.S. International Students and Scholars,* Institute of International Education, www.cies.org/about_fulb.htm.
- *Graduate Study and You,* Council of Graduate Schools, www.cgsnet.org/Default.aspx?tabid=163.
- *Scholarships, Grants & Prizes 2009 (Peterson's Scholarships, Grants & Prizes),* available at bookstores and on www.amazon.com.
- *The Grants Register 2010,* Palgrave, an imprint of St. Martin's Press LLC, www.palgrave.com/Products/title.aspx?pid=294924.
- *Ultimate Scholarship Book 2010: Billions of Dollars in Scholarships, Grants & Prizes,* Gazelle Book Services, www.supercollege.com/store/store.cfm.

Financial Aid Scams

Every year, thousands of graduate students seeking financial aid are victims of financial aid scams. To help protect students and their families from this type of rip-off, Congress passed the College Scholarship Fraud Prevention Act of 2000, Pub. L. No. 106-420, 114 Stat. 1867 (2000) on November 1, 2000. Among its provisions is a requirement that the U.S. attorney general, the secretary of education, and the Federal Trade Commission jointly submit to Congress each year a report on fraud by businesses or individuals that market advice or assistance to students and parents seeking financial aid for higher education. The act and the subsequent annual reports to Congress have done much to create awareness of financial aid frauds and scams.

Operators of deceptive and illegal financial aid operations frequently claim that they can provide better access to financial aid or provide more money than students can obtain through their own efforts. When seeking financial aid, be wary of services that claim to know of untapped sources or are aware of billions of dollars in unclaimed scholarship or financial aid, or claim to have very high success rates for securing financial aid. Look carefully at companies providing "testimonials" from satisfied customers, or being endorsed by various businesses, federal or state agencies, colleges or universities. The claims are often red flags and should be viewed as indicators of possible scams.

Be particularly wary of programs claiming fees for help with preparing financial aid forms and documents. The Higher Education Opportunity Act (HEOA), P.L. 110-315, enacted on August 14, 2008, contains strong protections for students and their families related to persons and entities providing student aid consultative or preparation services. This act requires that preparers disclose their identity on the Free Application for Federal Student Aid (FAFSA) and that they provide notice that the FAFSA is a free form and that any Web sites used by the preparer contain a link to the Department of Education's FAFSA Web page.

Other telltale signs of a possible scam are when you are asked to pay an application fee, no matter how small it may be, for administrative or overhead expenses. Legitimate scholarship or financial aid companies and preparers do not ask for payments of this type.

If asked to pay origination fees, default fees, or other upfront fees, be careful, as this may be another indication of a fraudulent or illegal operation. These fees are usually deducted from the loan payment check that you will receive.

The Federal Trade Commission provides the following tag lines as indicators of possible scholarship scams:

"The scholarship is guaranteed or your money back."
"You can't get this information anywhere else."
"I just need your credit card or bank account number to hold this scholarship."
"We'll do all the work."
"The scholarship will cost some money."
"You've been selected by a 'national foundation' to receive a scholarship"
"You're a finalist" in a contest you never entered.

If there are doubts regarding the legitimacy of the company or individual seeking to provide assistance, check with the financial aid officer of the college or university you are interested in attending or with the Better Business Bureau (www.bbb.org).

Graduate School Financial Aid Checklist

Here are some guidelines that will help when applying for the different types of financial aid:

_____ Apply for a U.S. Department of Education personal identification number (PIN). You will need a PIN to electronically sign your FAFSA. Online submission of the FAFSA is the fastest way to process your application. Apply at www.pin.ed.gov.

_____ Complete the most recent Free Application for Federal Student Aid at www.fafsa.ed.gov.

_____ Check your Student Aid Report (SAR) from the Department of Education. The SAR is the report sent by the Department of Education with the information from your FAFSA. You will receive your SAR either by e-mail or postal service, depending on whether you completed the FAFSA online or on paper. You should receive your SAR within four weeks of completing the FAFSA.

_____ Complete the Federal Stafford Loan Master Promissory Note (MPN) (optional). This application is required if you wish to borrow from the Federal Stafford Loan Program.

_____ Complete the Federal PLUS Loan for Graduate/Professional Students (optional). This application is required if you wish to borrow from the Federal PLUS Loan Program.

_____ Complete the Loan Entrance Counseling interview. Federal regulations governing the borrowing of federal student loans require that all students receiving a Federal Stafford and/or a Federal Grad PLUS Loan must complete this interview, which explains your rights and responsibilities as a borrower. For your convenience, the Loan Entrance Counseling program information will be linked to your Federal Stafford and/or Grad PLUS MPN application process. NOTE: You are also required to complete an exit counseling interview once you graduate or "exit" from your program.

_____ Apply for Veteran's Educational Benefits (optional). For information on the Post-9/11 Veterans Educational Assistance Act of 2008 or the "New GI Bill," visit www.gibill.va.gov and submit all required documents requested by the Veterans Administration.

_____ Choose a bank to loan the funds to you. It is preferable that you select the same lender that you have for your Stafford Loan, but this is not mandatory. You are free to select any bank you wish.

_____ Check for possible state sources of funding. A good starting place is http://wdcrobcolp01.ed.gov/Programs/EROD/org_list.cfm?category_cd=SHE.

_____ Check with your employer for tuition aid or other sources of financial assistance.

_____ Consult with family, friends, and relatives for possible loans.

_____ Check for other sources of private funds at www.fastweb.com.

4

THE DEGREE PROGRAM

> In my job, it is necessary to get a graduate degree in order to maintain my credibility. I never believed I could complete a program of study and still perform my professional responsibilities well. Besides, I never scored well on standardized tests, and the GRE was an admission requirement for the program I was interested in.
>
> After much coaxing, I took the GRE and was admitted. I'm not spending as much time as I want with my family and I can't spend the weekend watching football or my favorite sitcoms. But it feels so good to be accomplishing my educational goals. My self-respect and my credibility have never been greater.
>
> —*Fred*

A recurring theme throughout this book is the need to be aware of and to be in control as much as possible of every part of the graduate school process. No one cares more about your success than you do.

In this chapter, developing and completing the program of study are discussed. Specific information, activities, suggestions, and tips about accreditation; the many different types of degree programs; credits required for graduation; different types of courses; course delivery formats; program development; course completion; time management; controlling frustration; and the relationship of the mind, body, and spirit to program completion are presented.

Accreditation

An important concern about being in the right degree program relates to the accreditation of the degree. Accreditation is complex. The need to be an informed consumer is very important when seeking an advanced degree. Why is this?

Accreditation is a voluntary process conducted by private, nonprofit organizations designed to review and scrutinize colleges and universities and the programs within their purview. It is the primary way in which quality assurance and quality improvement of the college, university, or program is determined. There is no "centralized" federal agency that approves all degrees and/or programs. Accrediting agencies recognized by the Council for Higher Education Accreditation (CHEA) or the U.S. Department of Education operate on the local, state, regional, and national levels. In the United States alone, colleges and universities are accredited by one of nineteen recognized institutional accrediting organizations. Programs are accredited by one of approximately sixty recognized programmatic accrediting organizations.

There are four types of accreditation: *Regional* (New England Association of Schools and Colleges, North Central Association of Colleges and Schools, Middle States Association of Colleges and Schools, Southern Association of Colleges and Schools, Western Association of Schools and Colleges, and Northwest Commission on Colleges and Universities), *National faith-based* (i.e., Association for Biblical Higher Education, Commission on Accreditation of the Association of Theological Schools in the United States and Canada), *National career-related* (Accrediting Council for Independent Colleges and Schools and Distance Education and Training Council), and *Programmatic* (i.e., the Association to Advance Collegiate Schools of Business, the Accreditation Board for Engineering and Technology).

Accreditation is required for access to federal funds such as student aid and other federal financial assistance programs. Federal student aid funds are available to students only if the institution or program they are attending is accredited by a recognized accrediting organization. Many state funds also require accreditation before approving grants or loans to students. It is common for employers to require that the program be accredited before proving employee tuition assistance.

Although the acceptance of credits from one institution to another is the prerogative of the receiving institution, transferring credits is much easier if both the sending and receiving institutions are accredited. Many accredited institutions will not accept transfer credits from unaccredited institutions or programs no matter how hard you have worked to earn the credits or how closely they might relate to existing courses within the receiving institution.

To determine the accreditation status of a particular university, college, or program, contact the institution directly. Ask not only if the college, university, or program is accredited but also for the name of the accrediting agency. If the program is not accredited by one of the agencies recognized by the Council for Higher Education Accreditation (CHEA) or the U.S. Department of Education, or if the person you are speaking with cannot answer in a positive manner, carefully consider your reasons for wanting to enroll in this program. Once you have identified the accrediting agency, you can find out if it is a recognized agency by checking www.ed.gov/admins/finaid/accred/index.html.

Am I in the Right Graduate Degree Program?

Throughout the world, more than 120 varieties of master of arts (MA) degrees and 270 varieties of master of science (MS) degrees are offered. In the United States alone, accredited colleges or universities award more than 300 *different* graduate (master's and doctoral) degrees. It is important that you are in the right degree program for you.

A careful reading of the graduate catalog from almost any graduate school will reveal that the degree is awarded on the recommendation of the faculty offering the graduate degree. The traditional way of categorizing graduate degrees as being primarily research oriented or professionally oriented is no longer valid. At one time the PhD degree was defined as a research-oriented degree, and all other doctoral degrees were professionally oriented. Today, the difference between the PhD and other doctoral degrees (i.e., EdD, DBA, PsyD, etc.) are often indistinguishable. The degree is usually defined by a specific *degree title,* that is, master of arts (MA), master of business administration (MBA), master of science (MS), doctor of philosophy (PhD), doctor of education (EdD), and so on, and a *specialization* (often referred to as a major or concentration). It makes sense to know the exact degree title and specialization that will be awarded before you commit to a program of study. For example, verify in advance that you are working toward a PhD with a specialization in clinical psychology or an MA with a specialization in elementary education rather than *assuming* that this is the degree and specialization to be awarded upon graduation.

Certain professional degrees, such as the educational specialist (EdS) or the certificate of advanced graduate studies (CAGS), fit between the master's and the doctorate. It sometimes is not clear or obvious if these are degrees or certificates. In some cases, the university or college grants one as a degree with the same full rights and privileges attached to any other graduate degree. In others, the college or university grants a certificate that certifies completion of a prescribed program of study but is not an earned degree. It is very important to check with the graduate school to be sure you are enrolled in the correct degree and specialization or major.

Defining the Program of Study

To make the correct decisions about the program of study, it might be helpful to think about it in terms of academic credits. Some programs award credits based on the *semester* system whereas others award them based on the *quarter* system. Generally speaking, three semester credits equal four quarter credits. For the remainder of this section, we'll be talking about semester credits. To convert semester credits into quarter credits, multiply the number of semester credits by 1.25.

Credits Required for Completing Graduate Degree Programs

Type of Degree	*Number of Credits*
Master's degree (i.e., MA, MS)	30–36
"Terminal" master's (i.e., MBA, MSW)	60
Doctorate (i.e., PhD, EdD)	90

Although programs vary regarding the number of credits required for a master's or doctoral degree, a general rule to follow is that a master's degree requires the completion of 30–36 credits. Exceptions to this rule are those master's degrees that are considered "terminal," which may require sixty or more credits to complete. Examples of terminal degrees are the master of social work (MSW) and the master of counseling (MC) degrees. The doctorate, including the dissertation, usually requires about ninety credits.

Time Required to Complete Graduate Degrees

Type of Degree	*Average Time Required*
Master's degree (30–36 credits)	1 year full-time
"Terminal" master's (60 credits)	2 years full-time
Doctorate (90 credits)	3 years full-time

Another way to think about this is that a minimum of one year of full-time post baccalaureate study is generally required to complete the master's degree. Terminal master's degrees (i.e., MSW or MBA) may require a minimum of two years of full-time study. Completion of the doctoral degree usually requires a minimum of three years of full-time study.

Ideally, the graduate school has designed its graduate degree programs to reflect its own mission, which along with its goals and objectives are usually described in a separate section of the graduate school catalog. The various degrees offered by the institution should clearly relate to the mission of the graduate school and/or department. Most graduate colleges and departments implement the mission and purpose through their graduate degrees and programs of study.

In many schools, the program of study is a predetermined series of courses (offered either in the traditional classroom manner, through the online delivery format, or in a blended combination of both), followed by a comprehensive examination or other culminating experience such as a thesis, dissertation, or other research or application project. Although most doctoral degree programs require a dissertation of some sort, it is common for many master's degree programs not to have a thesis or any other final experience (see Chapters 5, 6, 7, and 8 for more information on the committee structure, comprehensive exam, thesis, and dissertation).

Following are the different categories of courses that are common in most graduate programs:

- Foundation or core (usually required of everyone in the program)
- Specialization (usually required for specializations or majors)
- Electives
- Field experience (practicum or internship)
- Independent study (individualized, one-on-one study)
- Final project/thesis/dissertation

It is normal for graduate programs to require that all graduate students in the department, regardless of their major or concentration, take a series of foundation courses known as *the core.* The thinking behind this is that the university and the faculty want to be assured that every student has been exposed to a common base of knowledge as it relates to the mission of the university or department, certain core concepts, principles, or ideas. An example would be a college of education requiring everyone at the master's level to take such courses as "The History and Philosophy of Education," "Introduction to Research," and "Field Experience" (sometimes called a *practicum* or *internship*), regardless of the concentration area selected. This ensures that every person completing a program of study in the college has at least been exposed to a common set of assumptions, knowledge, and literature related to the background and principles of education and research and will have an opportunity to apply information gained from the program of study in a "real-life" setting.

The scope and sequence of core courses or experiences usually have been developed by the faculty to reflect areas its members believe are important. These courses frequently begin with an overview of the field and are designed to provide breadth of information. These are also usually the department courses with the greatest enrollment, as all students in the department are required to take them.

Core courses at the doctoral level are usually more advanced than those required at the master's level. At the doctoral level, faculty usually want to guarantee that the students have more in-depth exposure to basic knowledge, particularly as applied to research and/or other core requirements of the field or discipline. Although it is common for master's degree programs to require at least one course in statistics and another in research design, it is equally common for doctoral programs to require 9–15 credits (or more) to be taken in research and statistics as well as foundation and advanced courses in the discipline or field in addition to a practicum or internship experience.

In addition to core courses, a program of study usually consists of courses or experiences (i.e., practicum or internship) relating to the concentration or area(s) of specialization offered by the graduate program. These courses are frequently referred to as the "major" or "specialization" courses. Many graduate programs consider a major or specialization to be 21–24 credits.

The purpose of these courses is to provide the latest and most current information about specializations offered by the college or department. These courses usually are more focused and frequently follow a seminar format in which there is ample discussion among the professor and the class members.

The field experience (practicum or internship) is designed to provide a "hands-on" opportunity to apply information gained through course work or to acquire specific information needed to complete a specialization area. It is usually completed "on site" and involves a local on-site supervisor cooperating with a university professor. Doctoral programs frequently require students to enroll in more than one field experience.

Many graduate programs require that courses be taken in a predetermined sequence and won't allow registration for the more advanced courses unless the prerequisite courses have been completed and/or other requirements, such as a certain number of years of work or clinical experience and/or an appropriate background in research design or statistics have been met. When looking at the requirements of your program, be sure to carefully review all descriptive materials provided by the program as well as course descriptions in the catalog to see what, if any, prerequisites are required.

Working with a professor on a one-on-one basis is a form of course work frequently used in graduate schools. This is called *independent study* or *directed study.* This type of instruction frees the student from regularly scheduled class meetings throughout the semester. The purpose of an independent study class is to allow for the pursuit of individual interests or specializations under the direct supervision or guidance of a particular professor. It may also allow for the development of a specific aspect of the specialization that would interest relatively few graduate students in the program or department. Independent study courses are perfect vehicles to help clarify the thesis or dissertation topic.

The advantages of independent study are obvious: your learning objectives are the sole concern of the learning experience. Time is not wasted listening to lectures about things already known or listening to the professor responding to student requests to clarify a point that is perfectly clear to you. In an independent study course, you are the center of attention and your needs are immediately attended to.

There are also downsides to this seemingly utopian situation. Given the opportunity to pursue individual interests at your own schedule may create an obsession with the subject. Hours upon hours may be spent in the library or on the Web tracking down a very obscure point or bit of knowledge. Although this may be intellectually rewarding, don't lose perspective and waste your time going after an obtuse point when that time might have been better spent completing other requirements of the program of study.

Ron, a graduate student in his second-to-last semester of a PhD program with a specialization in adult education, provides a good illustration of how a practicum can produce very positive results. Ron was particularly interested in applying the various theories he had learned about adult development in a real situation. He negotiated with his major advisor and arranged to complete a practicum as a curriculum developer in a local adult learning center. It did not take Ron long to realize that the models in use for developing curricula were based on research with youth and children. Little thought or attention had been given to the concept that the center was educating adults, not tall grown-up children. Ron discussed this with his advisor and the administrators of the center and agreed to develop, field-test, and evaluate a new model based on principles of adult development. From Ron's point of view, this was an ideal experience in that he was able to apply his theoretical knowledge in a real setting, and the center was able to benefit from his expertise.

The practicum was the most meaningful part of Ron's graduate experience from another perspective as well. Not only was he able to develop, field-test, and evaluate his model, but the practicum helped identify additional literature related to his dissertation topic. From a very practical point of view, Ron was hired as the curriculum developer at the center once he finished his degree!

In some graduate schools, there are no predetermined courses whatsoever. The student consults with his or her advisor and determines the courses to be taken. These types of programs are very good for highly self-directed learners, those with a rich experiential backgrounds, or those who have a very good idea not only of what they want to learn but also of how they want to learn it. A clear sense of purpose and objectives, as well as good negotiating skills, are very helpful in this type of program. Learners need to fully discuss and be particularly adept at negotiating learning objectives with their committee or chairperson. They also need to be aware of their personal reasons for being in the program and how the suggested courses or other learning experiences will accomplish their personal learning objectives. Learners who need structure should seriously consider if this type of degree program best fits their learning style.

Electives are another part of most graduate programs of study. These courses are not required but are available to supplement individual needs or interests in specific fields. They usually provide a greater depth of understanding about the specialization and serve to round out the program of study. They should be selected with the advice of the committee chair or a member of the committee.

It is not uncommon for a graduate program to have advisors other than the faculty available to help with routine matters. Sometimes advisors are graduate students themselves, in which case they are a very good source of information about departmental courses, concentrations, specializations, and faculty members. They are usually in touch with other students and are part of "the network" or "grapevine" that thrives in most graduate schools. In some programs, advisors are staff members who are well versed in the mechanics of degree completion. In many programs, advisors are hired as staff, are trained as counselors, and have in-depth knowledge of the program and its requirements.

A word of caution is needed here as well: sometimes the student or staff advisor can be perceived as having more authority or knowledge than he or she really has. Remember that no matter how knowledgeable or well-intentioned these advisors may be, a fellow student or staff advisor is *not* your chair and does *not* have the authority to make decisions regarding the program of study.

Online Courses

Most colleges and universities now offer courses in an online as well as classroom format. Several offer the entire program of study via *distance education,* generally described as a learning situation in which learners and teachers are separated by time and space and in which communication is facilitated through print or some form of technology. Courses can be either synchronous or asynchronous. Synchronous instruction requires learners and teachers to participate at the same time with interaction done in "real time." Delivery modes for synchronous instruction may include interactive TV and videoconferencing. Asynchronous instruction offers greater flexibility because students may choose to participate when it is convenient to their schedules. Web-based instruction, e-mail, online discussion groups, videotapes, and correspondence courses are used in courses offering asynchronous instruction. Social networks such as Facebook, YouTube, and LinkedIn are gaining increasing use as supplements for online courses.

Online courses are a wonderful option and are most often viewed as a "win-win" situation for both you and the institution. You win most in that you control the time you spend working on the course. You can also save a great deal of time traveling to the university and determining when you will "attend" class.

There are downsides to these types of courses as well. For example, there are the added hardware costs associated with a computer. There are also the technical glitches that can cause frustration and anxiety for many learners. Also, it should be remembered that writing is an important aspect of online courses. Learners with poor writing skills often report that they feel intimidated or uncomfortable in online classes.

Additional questions and answers regarding online courses are presented in Chapter 2.

Developing and Completing the Program of Study

Every graduate school has its own way of developing and processing the program of study. This process is explained in the program of study material provided by the department or college. Some provide a packet of very formal written documents with a variety of examples, whereas others provide a list of dates and some blank forms that are refined or developed as needed. As with every bit of paperwork connected with your degree, it is very important that you know exactly what forms need to be filled out, when they are due, and who needs to approve them.

In almost every case, the program of study needs to be approved and signed by various college administrators or department faculty. These people may be members of the graduate committee, the department head, or representatives from the graduate college. It makes good sense to make an appointment and hand-carry your program of study forms to each of the required individuals for their signature. If you are in a distance-education program, it makes good sense to call or e-mail the signatory to tell him or her that the program of study is on the way. Why? If the signers are faculty members, this provides another opportunity to meet with or contact them and discuss how your goals and objectives relate to your program of study. It also gives them an opportunity to get to know you. The importance of getting to know your committee members and getting to be known by them can't be stressed enough. This is discussed further in Chapters 5 and 6. Another important reason is that a saved e-mail provides a paper trail in the event the document is lost or misplaced.

Along with knowing what forms need to be filled out and who needs to approve the program of study, consider how your goals and objectives can be met through the program of study. Questions such as the following will help clarify personal goals and objectives: "Why do I want this degree?" "How will it help me?" "Do I need more courses rather than another degree?" "Am I prepared to invest the necessary time, energy, and resources to obtain this degree?" "Am I comfortable with an online environment?"

Let's assume that you want a graduate degree for personal reasons and also want to become certified (or licensed) within your profession. This is a common goal of many individuals seeking to earn a graduate degree. It is up to you to know the specific courses or other requirements of the certifying or licensing agency related to your profession. This information is available through the state, county, or local office charged with this responsibility. In some cases, the professional organization can provide it. A Web search will quickly produce the agencies and contact points you are seeking. It is important to remember, however, that although the program of study may be sufficient for the graduate college to recommend you for certification or to sit for the licensing exam, the certificate or license is usually granted by the appropriate agency, not the graduate college.

Almost every certifying or licensing agency has unique or specific requirements that must be met. Some require documentation of a certain number of clock hours related to specific profession-related tasks or learning activities. Some require certain courses with exact prefixes or workshops from a specific professional organization. Others may not accept courses delivered online. Still others may require noncredit courses or continuing education units (CEUs) from accredited colleges or universities. Not only is it up to you to know the certification or licensing requirements, it is also to your advantage to think about how (and if) these requirements can be met through your program of study.

Keep personal goals and objectives clearly in mind as the program of study is developed. Ask yourself how each course or learning experience will help accomplish your goals.

Try to develop the initial draft of the program of study as much as possible without the assistance of your committee chair or advisor. Although this may seem foolish and a waste of time, it forces you to become very familiar with the various forms and policies governing the program of study. Often, new faculty members are not fully aware of the process and may give incomplete advice. The more experienced faculty members are less apt to give inaccurate or incorrect advice, but let's face it; they will generally give advice that reflects their style or their inclinations. They probably don't know you and your needs as well as you do. Perhaps this person is fairly set in his or her ways and doesn't look for options. This person, although well meaning, might not think about or consider alternatives. Having reviewed the program of study forms and the departmental and college policies and procedures, you understand how the system works. This provides you with a stronger rationale when seeking exceptions. The worst that can happen is that the request will be denied.

After you have completed an initial draft of the program of study as fully as possible, make an appointment to visit or call your committee chair. Using this draft as the basis of discussion, seek to discuss what you want to do rather than only requesting the chair's ideas about what you should do. All too often, graduate students fall into the traditional teacher-student role and give away their options by asking the advisor such questions as: "What courses should I take?" "What electives should I take?" "Should I take online courses?" "Who should I have on my committee?" You are in a much stronger position when you have thought about your program of study, discussed it with other graduate students, and developed tentative answers to your questions that you would like to discuss with your advisor.

For example, a more assertive rather than passive approach would be: "I want to take these courses, as they are not only core courses but they also fit into my personal plans. What do you think?" or "I think these electives are appropriate to my learning objectives and would like your advice on them. What's your opinion?" "I want to take several courses online. I feel this experience will be to my advantage, as online courses are the wave of the future. What's your reaction?" You want to avoid being in a position of not having considered the types of responses you want and then accepting responses that may not be the best ones in your specific situation.

If you have a draft in hand and have thought about the concerns as well as the solutions, this can enable you to better use the meeting to negotiate a program that more accurately reflects your needs and objectives. Tactfully handled, this type of negotiation can positively affect your committee chair and committee members in that it demonstrates that you not only have carefully thought about your reasons for being in graduate school but also have considered ways in which the program of study can facilitate your needs. This can psychologically change committee members' perceptions of you from the "traditional" student (one who comes to the teacher as a child comes to a parent) to that of a "mature" student (a confident individual seeking the advice of a peer).

Using this approach, students are more able to solicit advice based on specific needs and negotiate a program of study that more fully reflects these goals and objectives, rather than receiving the "cookbook" responses often given by faculty.

Once you have met with your chair, secured needed information, and negotiated responses acceptable to both of you, the next step is to revise the draft of the program of study and have it reviewed again by your committee chair. All that remains is for the other committee members and/or the department chair of the school to approve it.

Remember that the most important part of the process in developing the program of study is to carefully study the policies and procedures relating to the development of the program of study. Look for ways to accomplish your personal and professional objectives. This makes developing the program, seeking advice, and negotiating a program that is responsive to your particular concerns much easier.

Sample Program of Study Form

The following is a generic form that can be used to develop the initial draft of your program of study. It is suggested that you use this form or one supplied by your graduate program to complete a sample program. This should not be done until after relevant college and departmental policies and procedures have been studied and reviewed and faculty, staff, and fellow learners have been consulted.

Sample Program of Study

COURSES	*SEMESTER PLANNED*	*SEMESTER COMPLETED*
List all **Core** or **Required** courses here:		
1, 2, 3, etc.		
List all **Specialization** or **Major** courses here:		
1, 2, 3, etc.		
List all **Elective** courses here:		
1, 2, 3, etc		
List all **Independent Study** courses here:		
1, 2, 3, etc.		
Comprehensive exam		
Proposal developed		
Proposal completed		
First draft of thesis/dissertation completed		
Thesis/dissertation accepted		
Thesis/dissertation defended		

Recognize that the development of the program of study is a series of iterations in that it will probably be revised several times following consultation with others involved in the graduate degree process. In fact, this is the way it usually is done.

The completed program of study form should be considered a flexible rather than static document. It could change as a result of courses being added to the schedule that were not available when the program of study was initially developed. It might also be revised due to changes in the schedule that prevent the course from being offered at the time you originally wanted to take it. Perhaps you might want to extend the practicum or internship from one semester to two. The program of study should serve as a guide for planning how to meet academic and professional goals.

Most college and university graduate programs will use the approved program of study as the basis for an audit that determines if you have completed all courses and requirements and will be allowed to graduate. Thus, it is very important that the program of study be kept current and any changes recorded with the department or the office of the registrar.

Completing Course Work

Completing the courses on the program of study involves advance planning to fit the courses into your schedule. It also means completing classes, taking notes, preparing for exams, and completing required term papers and/or projects, as well as other class requirements. It might also mean scheduling time at home for you to be on the computer while taking an online class and not being available to your family. Regardless of how you do it, it means mastering course content.

A conscientious graduate student needs to understand how the courses fit in with personal reasons for being in graduate school. How do they relate to areas of research interest? What concerns have piqued curiosity sufficiently to be considered as possible research topics for the dissertation or independent study?

The proposal, thesis/dissertation, and oral defense are also considered part of the program of study. These are discussed more fully in Chapters 7 and 8. Ideally, these culminating experiences evolve from the completion of the course work listed in the program of study. The connections between the courses and literature being reviewed for course term papers and the thesis/dissertation are logical and easy to see. When the connections have been made, the graduate student can make an easy transition from taking courses to writing the final product.

If grades are important, be attuned to the subtleties of the course and seek to understand the little things that are important to the professor in addition to the course objectives and requirements presented in the syllabus. It is quite possible to determine if the professor values discussion by the way in which questions or requests for elaboration are handled. If this seems to be valued, it makes sense to ask meaningful questions and thoughtful requests for elaboration. However, be tactful, as this can be viewed as a bid for attention and can be counterproductive if not handled carefully. If discussion is not valued by the professor, the astute graduate student will find other ways to get answers to questions without jeopardizing the grade by unwittingly being antagonistic or overly aggressive.

Know Yourself

You are one of your most important resources. You consist of a mind, a body, and a spirit. There is much to be said regarding the interconnectedness of the mind, body, and spirit and their relationship to completing a graduate degree.

The Mind

There is relatively little hard data about how the mind functions. We are sure, however, that each person's mind is unique and that each of us learns in a variety of ways. Some learn best from a lecture. Others prefer reading. Still others prefer to interact with material and contemplate the implications on a personal level. This notion is not new. The ancient Hindus viewed the different learning styles of people as active, passive, emotional, and thoughtful. The *Bhagavad Gita,* one of the holy books of the Hindus, suggested that these four learning elements were the four basic yogas, or pathways, needed to practice religion.

Psychologists and learning theorists have proposed a variety of theories to describe learning styles and how the mind processes learning; however, there is still no agreement on this. Researchers are still trying to formulate an acceptable definition of learning and the psychological, emotional, and volitional factors that affect learning.

The Body

Keeping in good physical shape is another way of ensuring completion of the graduate program. Most graduate students only think about the "mental" requirements when contemplating their degree. The "physical" side of the equation is equally important as well.

When reading textbooks or reviewing class notes in preparation for an exam, it is not uncommon to spend several hours in basically one position. This is hard on the body because blood circulation is restricted and muscles tend to tighten up. It also contributes to a feeling of being tired, which is a frequent lament of graduate learners.

The more sedentary one is, the less opportunity there is for adequate blood flow. Blood carries oxygen to all parts of the body. Without an adequate oxygen supply, there is a tendency to feel tired and listless. An easy solution is to make it a point to get up and walk around several times while studying. This allows for better circulation and may help avoid cramping and that tired feeling that often accompanies studying.

Another good way to recoup the energy lost while studying is to do something physical on a regular basis. Jogging or walking every day helps to keep the body in shape and one's energy level up. Joggers who also happen to be in graduate school frequently use running time as "think" time and have found jogging to be a good way to condition their body while using their mind. Many students find that a carefully planned exercise regimen at a local health and fitness club does wonders for maintaining the energy level required to complete a graduate program.

Playing racquetball or taking an aerobics or exercise class is another way of keeping in shape. Aerobic programs exercise the heart and lungs and assist these organs to better perform their vital functions. Any program designed to increase blood flow and oxygenation will result in greater energy levels.

Good nutrition is also important to completing a graduate program. There is ample evidence to suggest that good nutrition leads to healthier and longer lives. Good nutrition also increases powers of concentration. Although donuts and coffee might keep you awake and provide a temporary energy boost, they are not as effective in the long run as proper nutrition. A commercially prepared energy supplement low in calories and high in vitamins and nutrients does a more effective job in restoring needed energy.

As with any physical fitness or nutritional program, it is advisable to consult with a physician, dietitian, nutritionist, or other appropriate specialist to determine the best program for your individual needs.

The Spirit

The definition of *the spirit* is up to you. Some people define it as "the soul" and seek to develop it through meditation or religious activity. Others may define it as one's unique essence. What is being suggested here is that regardless of how the spirit is defined, it is important not to neglect it when completing the graduate program.

If you believe spirit is defined through a particular religious preference, don't forget about religion while engrossed in graduate studies. Stay true to your beliefs. There are many individuals who are firm in the belief that prayers do not go unanswered. If this is part of your religious belief system, don't let the stress of completing your program of study obscure the power of prayer. Use prayer if it will help relieve the stress and strain of graduate studies.

No discussion of the spirit would be complete without a word about keeping spirits up. It is important to remember that a graduate degree should be perceived as a means to an end, not the end itself. Many graduate students put too much stress on themselves by thinking that the world will end if they don't get the degree. Perhaps the only sure thing that can be said in this book is that, as of today, many graduate students have not gotten their degrees and, in spite of all the doomsday prophecies, the world has not ended.

Although it is important to recognize and acknowledge that a great deal of time, energy, and money is being invested in completing the degree, it is equally important to recognize that no matter how difficult it may seem, life will go on even if you do not complete the degree. Lighten up and have fun.

Controlling Frustrations

Life as a learner in graduate school can be a frustrating process. It is filled with very high "highs" and very low "lows." Graduate students constantly face uncertainties commonly associated with almost every graduate program that ever existed. In many ways, it is an emotional roller coaster.

The "highs" are times of absolute euphoria, such as "acing" a test, completing a truly wonderful term paper that draws the praise of your professor, passing the comps, having your proposal finally accepted, completing the thesis or dissertation, or best of all, graduating. These are the times when you see the light at the end of the tunnel and feel that the struggles are all worth it.

The "lows" are the times when you hate your faculty advisor, committee chair, committee members, the dean, the department chair, the professors, and everything and everyone remotely associated with your program. These times come when you are faced with situations over which you can exert little or no control, such as not knowing what material to study for the test, what will be on the comprehensive exam, sitting through a terribly boring course with an instructor who rambles on forever, or working in isolation on online courses. Equally frustrating times come when trying to get your committee to sign off on your proposal or trying to convince the department chair that the course taken before you transferred is the same one he now says needs to be retaken because it has a different prefix. These are the times you really want to scream, kick the dog, and yell at everyone!

There is also the general stress associated just with being in graduate school and being treated like a number rather than a person. Long lines at registration, computer breakdowns, not knowing what will happen after graduation, and wondering how to get the money for next semester's tuition are common stresses in the life of a graduate student.

A frequent frustration of graduate learners relates to faculty members returning the thesis or dissertation for revisions and seemingly being either unaware or unconcerned about the emotional distress this is creating. When this is discussed with the professor, a common response is that the revisions are needed to make the document as good as it can be. "After all," the faculty member says, "I have been through this many times before and I know what is needed to make this academically acceptable. Trust me." How can you argue with this? After all, the professor does have expertise and experience in this sort of thing. You do not. Even so, it is a frustrating experience and one that almost every graduate student will encounter.

A good bit of advice when you are experiencing frustration associated with a particular issue is to allow some time to pass before dealing with the issue. The passage of time helps reduce frustration.

As the author of this book, I can relate to frustration. After a contract to publish one of my other books was signed, my editor made several suggestions for improving the manuscript. I made them and sent in the revised manuscript, thinking that I was done with revisions. Not so! In fact, the book was substantially revised many times after the contract to publish was signed. Each time, my initial reaction was to think: "Oh, come on! Not again! It's fine the way it is! It doesn't need any further revisions. After all, I know what I'm talking about." I was frustrated.

However, following my own advice, I let some time pass before responding to the suggestions. This distanced me from my frustration and helped me realize that most of the suggestions really did improve the book. I was able to negotiate the changes once I had dealt with my frustrations.

It needs to be stressed that it is perfectly normal for the lives of graduate learners to be filled with many frustrations and upheavals. More important is finding ways to control them.

"RID": How to Control Frustration

1. **R**ecognize that you are frustrated.
2. **I**dentify the source of the frustration.
3. **D**eal realistically with the frustration.

The first step in dealing with frustration is to *recognize* you are experiencing frustration and admit it to yourself. Although this may sound very basic, it is not always easy to recognize and admit that you are frustrated. It is, however, key to do so. Many of us are pretty good at covering up our emotions, especially if we feel that to be emotional or frustrated is socially unacceptable or if we were conditioned to feel that adults shouldn't show their emotions. Thus, an important first step in controlling frustration is to admit being frustrated.

Once frustration is recognized, the next step is to carefully *identify* the true source of the frustration. This also is not as easy as it seems, because sometimes the source of the frustration is oneself, and this can be hard to accept. For example, have you ever blamed the noise the children were making when you were studying for your poor performance on a test when the real reason was that you simply didn't prepare sufficiently? Psychologists tell us that we frequently blame others for our shortcomings rather than accept the blame ourselves. Blaming others helps maintain self-esteem. To deal with frustration, the real source must be identified. Are you frustrated with your professor for making you revise the document, or are you frustrated with yourself because you don't want to do any more revising?

The final step is to *deal* realistically with the frustration. As mentioned earlier, a good approach is to let some time pass before confronting the source of frustration. During this time, develop a realistic plan of action for dealing with the frustration. Only you can decide what is realistic and reasonable, as only you can judge if it will work, given your knowledge of the situation.

As a general rule, if the source of frustration is another person, increased communication will probably help. If the source is yourself, you may need to find a way to release the frustration. Physical exercise, reading for pleasure, engaging in a hobby, or finding some other way to dissipate the pent-up frustration will help because frustration, like any form of energy, will not go away and needs to be released.

5

THE GRADUATE COMMITTEE

> Considering graduate school was difficult. I am a professor in a local college and I'm used to being in charge of my program. How could I let the professors at the "U" know that I didn't know everything and still keep my self-respect? Would I pick the right program? The right committee?
>
> Talking with colleagues, administrators, friends, and other students gave me some ideas about what might work for me. My doubts were reduced to workable challenges, and I was able to benefit greatly.
>
> —*Bill*

Perhaps the most important people in your entire graduate program are those who form your graduate committee. Collectively and individually, these individuals have a great deal of power related to the completion of your degree. Frequently, the committee will approve everything from the initial draft of the program of study through the final copy of the thesis or dissertation. Because the committee has real influence on your future, it is important to learn about the functions of the committee, its relation to the program of study, the different roles the various committee members play, and how to select an effective committee.

Functions of the Graduate Committee

The functions performed by the graduate committee vary from one college or university to another. In some instances the committee as a whole is intimately involved with every aspect of the graduate program. In other cases the committee serves as a "rubber stamp" for the committee chair, in that the chair makes most of the decisions and the committee does little other than approve them.

Most graduate committees perform one or more of these functions:

1. Approve the program of study
2. Develop and/or respond to the comprehensive examination
3. Approve the idea (or proposal) for the thesis or dissertation
4. Accept the final copy of the thesis or dissertation
5. Respond to the oral defense or presentation of the thesis or dissertation

The Program of Study

In Chapter 4 we discussed how to develop and complete the program of study. What is the role of the graduate committee in all of this?

In most universities, the graduate committee members can provide advice and direction beyond their official responsibilities and that which is readily available through routine printed matter such as graduate college catalogs or departmental guides. Realistically, members of graduate committees have been at the university longer than you have and can provide "behind-the-scenes" understandings of what can be done and what can't be done, what rules can be bent, and what regulations are inflexible. They are more aware than you of the subtleties of the committee process and may know how to maneuver and manipulate the process to mesh their teaching, research, and service objectives with your learning objectives and the objectives of the graduate program. These are the types of professors you want on your committee, because they know how the system works and will make it work for you.

They are important people to know for other professional reasons. Let's assume that Professor Barbara Smith is your committee chair and that the other members of your committee have been selected. More will be said about how to select committee members later in this chapter (see the section "Choosing Your Committee"). You have presented yourself well, are perceived as being competent, and seem to have a good rapport with committee members. In this situation, it is quite common for your chair and other committee members to take a professional interest in your success as a graduate student and as a professional in the field.

This manifests itself in a number of ways. For example, Professor Smith comes to know you and your abilities. She recognizes your potential. You appreciate her reputation and influence in the field. A natural outgrowth is that she becomes your mentor and begins a professional mentoring relationship that may last far beyond graduation.

In many universities, professors receive grants as one means of furthering their research and service agendas. If the relationship with your chair or other committee members is solid, it is not inconceivable that they would view you as a research assistant on one of their grants or would be willing to help you write a grant proposal of your own.

Perhaps one of the most important manifestations of a good relationship comes when you are looking for a job. This is when committee members and other faculty can help, particularly if they are well-connected and respected in their fields. It is amazing how many graduates find a new position or are promoted as a direct result of action by a professor.

What is not so obvious is that some professors know how the system works better than others. Those who are less adept at this often are usually less willing to do anything other than to perform routine committee functions in the traditional, time-honored manner. These individuals usually operate "by the book" and don't allow you much room to maneuver. Their style is rather predictable and pedantic, which is not necessarily bad. Although they won't work against you, they won't particularly work for you either.

It doesn't take much more than reading the provided department materials and talking with veteran students to know what the full committee needs to approve and what it doesn't. When signatures are required as proof of approval, be certain to obtain them yourself. Don't rely on other committee members to get them. They are busy and, even with the best intentions, they may not get it done. After all, it's your program. You need to be certain that everything that needs to be done is done. Don't take a chance and leave it to someone else, no matter how willing he or she is to take this task on. You need to protect yourself in the all too often bureaucratic graduate school world.

If each committee member needs to sign off to indicate approval of the program of study, use this as a time to meet with this person to discuss and negotiate, where possible, your program of study. Discuss any unusual, different, or extraordinary courses, practica, internships, field experiences, or other learning experiences.

Faculty members are usually busy people. In addition to their work on your committee, they have other responsibilities such as teaching, research, and service activities. These additional obligations make it difficult for some professors to give as much time to you as they would like. You may feel short-changed and resentful. It is not that they have forgotten what it was like to earn a graduate degree. They really are busy!

Respect the value of their time and don't waste it. Try to get answers first by reading the manual or catalog and speaking with a graduate advisor or others in the program; then, if necessary, confirm your answers with your committee.

Not only does this save time, it also makes you appear to be in more control of your program.

Comprehensive Examination

Quite often, the members of the graduate committee are responsible for preparing and responding to (grading) your comprehensive examination (a.k.a. comps). In Chapter 6 we will discuss the comps in detail. But for now, it is sufficient to say that the comps consist of a written and/or an oral component and are designed to demonstrate competency regarding the program of study. The comprehensive exam frequently serves as a "rite of passage" in that once it is successfully completed, the doctoral student is usually admitted to candidacy and can begin work on the thesis or dissertation. For master's students in nonthesis programs, completion of the comps is tantamount to graduation.

Often, graduate schools ask that committee members supply the questions for the comprehensive exam. In this situation, it is very important that members of your committee know you and your strengths and weaknesses. Taking this into account, it is a good idea to make an appointment to meet individually with committee members to seek their advice about the content of the exam. If you are taking your program online and this isn't possible, make telephone appointments with committee members. Be direct regarding your concerns, yet also be tactful. The worst thing that can happen when asking for advice about the questions on the comp is to be told nothing. Even in this worst-case scenario, you still have gained something, as you have created another opportunity to interact and negotiate with your committee.

Committee members recognize that it is virtually impossible to prepare for everything that might appear on a comp. In this spirit, it is not uncommon to receive fairly direct and succinct responses when asking what to study and how to prepare for the exam. For example, when talking with committee member X, you might be lucky and be given the areas of concern that this professor usually develops into comp questions. In your meeting with Professor Smith, you might learn that she feels class exams are her way of emphasizing major concepts or strategies. This is an extremely valuable bit of information, as she virtually has told you what to review. In these best-case scenarios, you not only have met and/or talked with your committee members but also have saved a lot of time and unnecessary worry.

Committee members frequently have the task of determining the form and content of the oral exam as well as the written one. It should be noted that not all comps have an oral component. At the oral, committee members may ask for elaboration or clarification of a response on the written part of the exam. In some graduate programs, a completely different set of questions are asked during the oral exam, because committee members may want to see how the student processes the question before responding or how well he or she acts and responds under pressure.

On one occasion, a very bright and very verbal doctoral student (let's call him Joe) was taking his oral comprehensive exam in anthropology. It was scheduled to run from 1:00 to 2:30 p.m. Three of the four committee members had another exam later that afternoon. Joe knew he had done well on the written comp and was expecting few problems on the oral.

Joe was quick to respond and gave long, obtuse responses when brief, direct answers were called for. Joe thought he was in control and doing a great job of controlling the oral by limiting the number of committee questions with his long and involved responses. What he didn't realize was that the committee members were becoming angry with him for wasting valuable time. About an hour into the exam, the committee chair stood up and dramatically interrupted one of Joe's long-winded responses by announcing that the committee had a series of questions that needed to be asked and that they would be asked and answered now! Furthermore, he said that the exam would end in thirty minutes and that if Joe did not respond to each and every question, he would probably fail the exam. Joe had totally misread the committee. Fortunately, he was able to recover and made the rest of his answers more concise. The committee members were able to ask their questions in the remaining time, and Joe passed the exam. He had almost failed because he did not understand the style of his committee members or the requirements of the comp. He should have discussed this process more carefully with his committee chair.

At many colleges, another function of graduate committees is to evaluate or grade the exam. In others, the exam is graded by a team of professors who do not know the names of the individuals whose exams they are grading. The rationale behind this type of grading is to reduce bias and increase inter-rater reliability.

It is vital that you understand the grading options in your school. For example, some schools have the "two chances" rule, which basically means that you have two chances to pass the comp. If you fail both exams, you are out. Others have other options. As a concerned learner, you need to know what options are in place in your school so that you can better prepare yourself for the comps.

Committee members may also have options related to grading or deciding the results of your comp. It is best for you when the committee members are unanimous in their decision to pass you on your comps. This signals full support and recognition of the successful completion of this phase of the program and gives tacit approval to begin work on the thesis or dissertation.

The committee may decide on a "provisional" pass. This means its members have concerns with a candidate's performance on the exam. If this happens, it is very important to check with each committee member for an explanation of what went wrong and the specific concerns of each committee member. This calls for a series of careful, tactful, and well-planned meetings with each committee member.

The worst result is a vote of failure on the comp. Although this is not a frequent occurrence, it does happen. If it happens to you, it is imperative to talk with your committee chair, your department head, and/or the graduate college to determine your options.

The Proposal, Thesis, and/or Dissertation

Information about the proposal, the thesis, and the dissertation is presented in considerable detail in Chapter 7. Committee members provide advice and assistance regarding the development of these parts of the graduate program of study. They usually enjoy this function more than evaluating the comp, as it is less stressful for all concerned.

Throughout this chapter, the importance of becoming known by your committee members and of them getting to know you has been stressed.

The better you, your style, and your ideas are known to the committee, the better will be the level of communication and understanding. The more time and effort expended on this, the easier for the committee to understand your intentions and to provide relevant, appropriate advice.

Roles of Committee Members

On most graduate committees, there is a chairperson (frequently referred to as the major advisor) and from one to four other members. It is not uncommon for master's committees to have fewer members than doctoral committees. Depending on the policy of the graduate program, committee members are usually appointed either by the graduate college or by the department head. Many programs will seek your recommendation regarding potential committee members as part of the selection process. Before final appointments are made, the administration and proposed faculty frequently consult to ensure an equitable distribution of the departmental workload, compatibility with the student, faculty interest, and to assure that both content and research expertise are available to the student.

You can and should play an integral part in the selection of your graduate committee members. As always, be sure to follow the university or department policies and procedures governing the establishment of the committee. If there are no formal policies, be certain to know when the committee is formed, how it is formed, the number of required members, and the functions of each member. Even if it is not part of the process, it makes sense to formalize your suggestions regarding potential committee members and send your recommendation in writing to the administrator or professor who has final responsibility for making committee selections. The worst that can happen is that your recommendations will be ignored. At best, your suggestions might help in securing a committee that you feel will be best for you. Nothing ventured, nothing gained!

In varying degrees, each committee member's roles and responsibilities, as shown in the following list, are:

1. To advise you regarding course selection, program development and completion, the comprehensive exam, the proposal, and the thesis or dissertation
2. To direct your work regarding independent study, the practicum, and/or the internship
3. To supervise your work as a teaching or research assistant
4. To provide assistance regarding job prospects

Chairperson or Major Advisor

Probably the most important person in your graduate school life is the *chairperson* or *major advisor* of your committee. There is no single job description that adequately defines this role. Clearly, such things as the prevailing policy of the department or college and the temperament, style, experience, research expertise, and concern of the individual all come into play when discussing this function. As mentioned earlier, this person may serve as a mentor and may be quite influential in helping you secure financial aid and in finding a job after graduation. In many colleges and universities, the committee chair forcefully directs the entire process, whereas in others, he or she facilitates rather than directs. It is obviously in your best interest to determine the operational style of your chair.

In almost every university, faculty members exercise a great deal of autonomy. How they teach, supervise, chair, coordinate, direct, or facilitate is based on their experience and understanding of their position, regardless of what is stated as policy. The same holds true regarding their roles as committee members and committee chairs. Whether this is right or wrong is not the issue. It is frequently a fact of graduate college life and one you have to understand and live with.

Few, if any, committee chairs have ever had any formal training or preparation for this role. The prevailing feeling seems to be that having gone through a similar program as a graduate student, having completed a graduate degree, having served on graduate committees, or having been appointed to the graduate faculty is sufficient preparation for serving as a committee chair. Although this may seem inefficient, this has been going on for years and can be used to your advantage, as is shown later in this chapter (see the section on "Choosing Your Committee").

Regardless of the way in which your committee chair functions, you need to do a great deal of listening, discussing, and negotiating during this process. The vast majority of graduate departments have never given thought to training chairs on how to listen, how to lead, or how to reconcile differences. Most faculty members acquire this knowledge by working with students and asking questions of their colleagues. Trial and error serves as a good teacher. Those who take this role seriously become good at it in a relatively short time. Once their reputations become established, they are sought out, as they are known to be helpful, knowledgeable, student oriented, and competent.

There are faculty members who really don't like being on committees. They see this function as taking time from their other university interests and responsibilities such as research, publishing, or personal outside interests. Others feel that current teaching, research, and service responsibilities leave them little time for advising. They may view advising as too time consuming and resent the intrusion. The grapevine is usually quite active about these faculty, but unfortunately, this does not prevent them from being assigned as a committee chair or member.

Regardless of whether or not your chairperson has a wonderful or a horrible reputation, the chairperson has power and needs to be treated with respect. Realize that without the cooperation of the committee chair, it will be difficult to complete your program. This does not mean acquiescing to each and every suggestion that is made, but it does suggest a need to carefully, skillfully, and tactfully negotiate with your chair. For each suggestion that is made, ask yourself questions such as these: "Is it a valid point?" "How much will it improve my work?" "What additional work will I need to do to incorporate the suggestion?" and "What will I gain or lose if the suggestion is questioned?" The advantages and disadvantages of questioning the advice or suggestion of any committee member, especially the chair, must be given top priority and be very carefully considered.

Other Committee Roles

Of lesser importance are the roles of the other committee members. This is *not* to say that the other committee members are not important. Clearly they are. Just as you would carefully listen to your committee chair, the views, thoughts, and suggestions of the other committee members need to be very carefully considered throughout the process for you to succeed and retain control of your graduate school odyssey.

The roles of committee members lend themselves to the purpose of the committee—to provide advice and assistance regarding the completion of the program of study. To accomplish this, committee members may be assigned to your committee based on their knowledge of process, research, and/or content.

This means that a committee member who possesses knowledge of the research process may be assigned to your committee to ensure that at least one committee member can provide expert advice regarding research design or methodology. Another member may be assigned based on knowledge of specific content. In this way, at least one committee member has content expertise and can be relied on to provide this assistance as needed.

Committee membership based on differing functions creates a system of checks and balances and may help avoid a committee that is dominated by the committee chair or a particularly strong-willed member. Soliciting advice and opinions from all committee members also may help avoid dominance by one member, as this helps to ensure that all committee members have a stake in the process. It also may provide different opinions regarding appropriate research design, course selection, or other program variables.

As part of the checks and balances system, many graduate school deans assign a dean's representative to the committee. This person usually provides little in terms of process and content advice and mainly is assigned to ensure that quality control standards of the college or university are adhered to strictly and impartially.

Getting to Know Potential Committee Members

It makes very good sense to know your committee because, regardless of whether its members have been appointed or you have selected them, or whether they have developed the comprehensive exam questions, they have a major impact on the outcome of the exam.

The easiest way to do this is by enrolling in the course(s) of department professors who may be eligible to become members of your committee. If the course(s) are part of the program of study, this not only fulfills a program requirement but also provides an opportunity to observe this person in action. During the term or semester, personal concerns, areas of expertise, research interests, peeves, pet projects, and topics of interest will be mentioned. Be sure to note these when they are identified.

Noting these concerns is a good idea even if the person does not become a committee member, as it can result in a better understanding of the goals and objectives of the course. It also is a good way to gain insights into those things that are important to the instructor. Knowing this may result in a better grade.

While in the course, try to get a feel for this person as a committee member. How well do you think he or she would respond to your ideas or interact with the other potential members of your committee? How do you feel about this person as a possible committee chair?

Becoming Known by Potential Committee Members

Being in a course offered by a potential committee member is a two-way street because it not only gives you a chance to observe the professor at work but it also provides the professor an opportunity to get to know you as well. It is important to make a good impression. Give thoughtful answers to questions posed in class. Make certain your online postings demonstrate correct grammar and syntax. Make an extra effort to ensure that all class assignments are done in a timely manner and at a graduate level. Definitely don't be late for class. If anything, try to arrive a few minutes early. Whatever you do, don't doze off! If you are taking online classes using asynchronous discussion groups, post your responses early in the week and return often to comment on your classmates' postings.

Try to find legitimate reasons to interact with the instructor. One-on-one meetings, either in person or by phone, allow the professor to get to know you as more than a member of the class. Your strengths, your personality, and your individuality become known.

For example, the ability to compare, contrast, analyze, synthesize, and integrate information is a goal of most graduate education (see the section "Compare, Contrast, Analyze, Synthesize, and Integrate" in Chapter 6 for more information). This is often what differentiates graduate school from undergraduate school. You are well advised to use class discussion to develop and practice this skill.

Let's say that you are in a seminar in which there is ample opportunity for discussion. Used wisely, this is a great opportunity to demonstrate your ability to compare and contrast what is being presented with other relevant information, theories, or theorists known to the field. Also, use term papers, class presentations, or essay exams to demonstrate your ability to synthesize what has been written or discussed to develop a new idea or application. In online discussion forums, you usually have time to think about your response before you post it. Take advantage of this, as it will allow you to develop your responses more fully and adequately. These are the types of behaviors and responses that most graduate faculty are looking for. Once they realize you are capable of this type of response, they are more likely to view you as a competent professional and one on whose committee they might like to serve.

You will also find that when developing your thesis or dissertation, nobody wants your opinion unless it is backed up by references in the literature of your field. This is a sad fact but one that clearly applies at this stage of your program. Committee members want you to substantiate your opinion by comparing, contrasting, analyzing, synthesizing, and/or integrating it with the opinions, findings, and writings of experts. The skill you have developed in your courses and papers relative to this ability will only be to your advantage when writing and revising your dissertation.

Make yourself known within your department by volunteering to serve as a student representative if and when the opportunity presents itself. Participate in the online blogs sponsored by the department or school. Meet with the graduate dean, department chair, or various faculty to discuss aspects of the graduate program that you particularly like or feel may need clarification. If a staff member has been helpful to you, write a letter (with copies to appropriate supervisory personnel) thanking that person. When this type of assertive behavior is handled well, it goes a long way toward helping you become known as a real person rather than a number or simply "another graduate student." It can also help to ensure that your suggestions and comments relating to your graduate committee may be listened to as well.

When trying to become better known by your committee, be careful not to push too hard. Keep in mind that faculty have many responsibilities in addition to serving as a committee member. They are involved in their own research, teaching, and service activities and serve as committee members to many other learners.

The key to becoming known by your committee members is the careful, skillful, and tactful way in which you do it. Don't be too obvious. Keep in mind that faculty may recognize and resent being manipulated. Be mindful and respectful of their time. They have other obligations and value their time. Don't waste it.

Choosing Your Committee

It is vital to know the process by which committee members are selected or assigned. Speak with graduate advisors, fellow students, graduates, and faculty to obtain this information. Don't forget department staff as they deal with these details all the time and may have additional insights that might be quite useful to you. Be certain to obtain any and all brochures, handouts, or other material describing policy or procedures relative to committee selection and/or appointment. Use the online learner discussion groups. Once you have this information, use it wisely. Seldom, if ever, are students specifically prohibited from suggesting specific committee members. In fact, many administrators welcome your input because it can make the committee selection process smoother and more efficient.

A well-functioning committee is very important to the successful completion of your graduate program. It makes sense to take an assertive role in all aspects of committee selection. A key way to retain some control over this part of the program is to carefully consider those faculty members with whom you work well or those faculty with whom you have developed a good feeling about as a result of taking their course or observing how they interact with your peers. Feel free to suggest that they be assigned or appointed to serve on your committee.

There is no "best" way to choose a committee. Each graduate college or department has its own policies and procedures for doing so. In some programs, the process is rather formal. Policy guides are provided, manuals are to be closely followed, checklists need to be checked off, forms need to be filled out, and rigid due dates are set for everything. Other programs operate in such a loose manner that it is a wonder that committees are ever formed! Still other programs combine form and process with creativity and encourage individuals to develop innovative programs that truly reflect individual needs and objectives.

Regardless of the type of graduate program you are in, it is very important to consider the qualities you are looking for in committee members. Don't be afraid to ask questions and to negotiate concerns with faculty. Don't operate on hearsay, rumors, or innuendo. Don't be persuaded by the advice of other students, regardless of how well intentioned they might be. Check it out for yourself. Do everything you need to do to really understand the process.

Become involved with the process at every level. Don't wait for things to happen. Take the initiative and make them happen. This might mean writing letters or e-mail messages suggesting potential committee members or otherwise consulting with your advisor, department head, or graduate dean to offer suggestions. Do whatever is necessary to achieve a committee that works well with one another, understands your learning style, and, perhaps most important, will work for your success.

Committee Member Selection Guide

The question frequently raised by graduate students when seeking committee members is: "How do I know what to look for in a potential committee member?" The Committee Member Selection Guide (CMSG) has been designed to help you determine which characteristics of effective committee members are important to you and the degree to which faculty demonstrate attainment of those characteristics.

The CMSG is a list of characteristics of effective graduate committee members as perceived by the graduate students that I have worked with throughout my career. This is not a definitive list, and no claims are made regarding its reliability or validity. It is included as an aid in collecting and evaluating information about faculty who might serve as members of your graduate committee.

Make copies of the CMSG on the following pages and complete one for each faculty member you are even remotely considering for your committee.

Committee Member Selection Guide (CMSG)

Directions: (a) In the blank before each characteristic of effective committee members, place an "*I*" if you feel this characteristic is *Important* to you OR place an "*N*" if you feel it is *Not important* to you. (b) Use the following rating scale for the second part of this activity.

0 = Absent or unable to determine

1 = Low attainment

3 = Moderate attainment

5 = High attainment

For those characteristics you have rated as "important," place a check mark (✓) above the appropriate number to indicate your perception of the degree to which the potential committee member has demonstrated attainment of that characteristic.

POTENTIAL COMMITTEE MEMBER

____

(NAME)

____ 1. Shows fairness	0	1	2	3	4	5
____ 2. Has a sense of humor	0	1	2	3	4	5
____ 3. Has subject matter expertise	0	1	2	3	4	5
____ 4. Shares my interests	0	1	2	3	4	5
____ 5. Is a good communicator	0	1	2	3	4	5
____ 6. Is a good negotiator	0	1	2	3	4	5
____ 7. Asks probing questions	0	1	2	3	4	5
____ 8. Knows the literature of the field	0	1	2	3	4	5
____ 9. Is professional in relationships	0	1	2	3	4	5
____ 10. Relates well to graduate students	0	1	2	3	4	5
____ 11. Considers individual differences	0	1	2	3	4	5
____ 12. Suggests ways in which information may be applied	0	1	2	3	4	5
____ 13. Is well prepared	0	1	2	3	4	5
____ 14. Motivates interest in learning	0	1	2	3	4	5
____ 15. Is well organized	0	1	2	3	4	5
____ 16. Is a good listener	0	1	2	3	4	5
____ 17. Is enthusiastic	0	1	2	3	4	5
____ 18. Is flexible	0	1	2	3	4	5
____ 19. Has good research skills	0	1	2	3	4	5
____ 20. Is experienced as a committee member	0	1	2	3	4	5
____ 21. Maintains office hours or is available to meet with students	0	1	2	3	4	5
____ 22. Is open and honest	0	1	2	3	4	5
____ 23. Is structured	0	1	2	3	4	5
____ 24. Is supportive	0	1	2	3	4	5
____ 25. Sets deadlines	0	1	2	3	4	5

Discussion: The CMSG provides a profile regarding your perceptions of the degree to which faculty members exhibit the characteristics of effective committee members. Characteristics rated 3 or higher are acceptable levels of attainment. Faculty members demonstrating “moderate” to “high” levels of attainment on those characteristics important to you probably would be effective committee members.

6

THE COMPREHENSIVE EXAM

> I was scared stiff at the thought of returning to school, taking courses, and having to pass exams. I never did well on written exams and, as a result, had some doubts about my ability to complete a graduate degree. Could I sit in class, take notes, write papers, and study for tests the same way I did when I was an undergrad?
>
> Well, I'm now in grad school and doing quite well. My family and I have discussed my concerns and we all have made the necessary adjustments. I'm preparing for my comps. I know it's only a matter of time before I graduate.
>
> —*Paulette*

Graduate programs frequently have something called a comprehensive examination, or "comp." The comp usually is taken during the last semester of course work or immediately after course work has been completed. In some programs, it is referred to as the "prelims" or "qualifying exam." It is designed to demonstrate competency and mastery of the program of study. Regardless of what it is called, it is a formal process and is generally considered to be the capstone experience regarding the course work you took as part of your program of study.

Many, but not all, master's degree programs have a comp. It is very unusual for doctoral programs not to have one. Comps are most often a written exam lasting anywhere from two hours to two days. Many schools follow the written exam with an oral exam that is designed to provide further evidence of competence and mastery of the program of study. Some have only an oral. For those graduate programs in which the comp is offered, passing it is a major milestone.

Graduate students approach the comp with a feeling of dread and fear. For many, the thought of this type of exam causes the body to ache and the mind to turn to mush. This perception is especially true for the learner who has a bachelor's degree, has been out of school for a number of years, and is thinking of returning to graduate school. Having completed an undergraduate degree, even with honors, does little to lessen the dread and fear. However, it is important to recognize that attainment of the bachelor's degree is indicative of success and demonstrates an ability to take exams regardless of how many years ago it was completed.

Purpose of the Comprehensive Examination

The purpose of the comprehensive exam is to demonstrate to the committee and the graduate college that you have mastered your program of study. This is its purpose at both the master's and doctoral levels.

In many doctoral programs, the comp determines whether the learner is ready to be admitted to candidacy. Being admitted to candidacy means that the learner has completed course work, has passed the comp, and is now ready to proceed with proposal development and completion of the dissertation.

Compare, Contrast, Analyze, Synthesize, and Integrate

When preparing for the comp, remember these five key words: *compare, contrast, analyze, synthesize,* and *integrate.* These intellectual skills are intended outcomes of all graduate education. The latter three skills are what frequently differentiates undergraduate from graduate education.

Compare: to determine similarities
Contrast: to determine differences
Analyze: to determine the relationship of the parts
Synthesize: to combine parts to make something new
Integrate: to unite the parts forming a new whole

In the comp, as well as in all graduate courses, it is important to look for ways of comparing or contrasting sources of information. Comp questions call for more than a rehash of information presented in class. For example, in graduate school a common assumption is that once an individual completes course work, basic knowledge from the program of study has been mastered. Therefore, at the comp, expect to be asked to discuss the similarities and differences (i.e., compare and contrast) between and among the various ideas, thoughts, concepts, trends, and/or patterns that were presented in the course. Or expect to be asked to analyze the relationship of the various parts of a particular theory or how the course material can be applied (i.e., synthesized or integrated) within your own profession. Prepare accordingly.

It makes sense to answer questions as much as possible by comparing, contrasting, analyzing, synthesizing, and integrating your response with information gained from courses and independent study. This is true for both the written and oral parts of the exam. More tips for responding to questions at an oral exam are presented in Chapter 8.

The Comprehensive Examination Process

Comprehensive examinations are usually given once course work has been completed but prior to the development of a final project or the development of the dissertation or thesis proposal. The comp may consist of a written exam, an oral exam, or both. At some institutions, the comp exam is individualized to reflect unique programs of study, but at others it may be a standardized exam developed by the faculty of the department or program. Regardless of which method is used, the questions seek evidence of competence regarding course work described in the program of study (i.e., the core, the specialization, and research).

It behooves you to know the operational policy relating to the number of times you can take the comp. In many schools, the "two chances and you are out" rule is in effect. This means that if you fail the first comp, there is usually a mandatory waiting period before you are allowed to retake the comp. It also means that if you fail a second time, there is usually no appeal and you are out of the program.

The Written Comp

When the comp is *individually* developed, usually the chair or major advisor prepares his or her own questions, obtains additional questions (usually from the committee members), and designs the comp. It is best if the examinee has completed a course or two with the committee members and has an idea of the concepts or ideas that are important to each. This is especially important if the program has been taken online, as you probably won't have many opportunities to meet face-to-face to discuss areas of concern. As discussed in Chapter 5, committee members usually ask questions reflecting their particular areas of interest and/or expertise. Knowing this gives a better idea of the nature of the questions that will be asked.

A *standardized* comp means that everyone takes the same exam at the same time on the same day. The standardized comp format attempts to ensure that everyone is treated equally and that no one has an advantage over anyone else. The dates for the exam are usually scheduled well in advance, and it clearly is your responsibility to know when the exam is scheduled. With standardized comps, the exam is usually drawn from a pool of questions developed over the years. The department head, the dean, or the program chair may appoint a committee charged with developing a new exam each year. Whatever the process, standardized exams are usually very stressful, as it is frequently more difficult to anticipate the questions.

After the written exam has been administered, it is rated, evaluated, or graded by the chair, by the committee members, or by a departmental committee. When the exam is reviewed with no knowledge of whose written exam is being read, it is referred to as being read *blind.* The readers do not know whose exam they are reading. When a department uses standardized exams, they are most often read blind.

The Oral Comp

Many graduate programs follow the written part of the comp with an oral part, but some do not. Just as there is no set way of developing or administering the written part, there is no set way of developing or administering the oral part. Nor is there any uniform way to determine the purpose or nature of the oral exam, the time provided between the written and the oral parts of the exam, or the circumstances when the oral may be optional or omitted. Make it your business to know these things as they apply to your school. Contact your committee chair, department head, graduate school counselor, or advisor either in person, by phone, or by e-mail. Check it out on the college or university Web page. If an oral exam follows the written exam, be sure to know when the oral is administered (one day following the written exam? one week later? two weeks later?) and the circumstances under which it is administered. Also make it your business to know, for example, if you are expected to make arrangements for the oral or if the department secretary or administrative assistant does this.

For a written exam with few, if any, errors of fact or interpretation, an oral does little to provide additional insight regarding competence and mastery of the program of study. This enlightened view may make the oral exam superfluous and is the reason why several graduate schools make the oral optional. Find out if your program has this option. If it doesn't, why not discuss this with your chairperson as a possibility? The worst that can happen is that it can't be done.

When an oral exam is required, its primary purpose is to provide a way for elaboration on what has been written or for an explanation of a point or statement that is not completely clear or correct. At the oral, the committee members ask whatever they want as it relates to your written exam. In some instances, questions are not drawn from the written responses and may not relate to the written questions at all.

Again, there are no set rules about this process. Do your homework and ask classmates who have been through it what it was like. Ask specific questions relating to both the process and the content.

Spend the time between the written and oral parts of the comp reviewing what you have written. Review the exam by looking for areas of weakness. Think of yourself as a committee member preparing to take part in your oral exam. This person will quite likely review the written exam to determine areas of weakness or areas in which elaboration is needed. Do the same thing. Ask friends, family members, or others whose opinions you value to review your written responses and look for the same things. This is particularly useful when a major part of a theory has been omitted or the work of one writer has been confused with that of another. Use the time to compare, contrast, analyze, synthesize, integrate, and otherwise review the literature and theories you may have omitted in your written exam. Make notes in the margins of the written exam paper and be sure to refer to this at the oral, if this is a part of the comp process in your school. Given that the examinee has written the material, most graduate schools allow you to have your written exam with you at the oral. However, check the policy guidelines to be sure this is permitted.

Evaluating the Comp

The evaluation process is usually completed within a reasonable time period. Different graduate schools have different ways of evaluating the comp. Some use a point system and award a certain number of points for each correct answer. Others use letter grades or grade them as "pass" or "fail." Still others rank the exams in some other way. It is important to know when to expect the results and what type of results to expect. If you fail, what are your options for retaking the exam? What special considerations, if any, are provided for learning disabilities such as dyslexia? Discuss this with your committee chair, dean, or learning disabilities coordinator before you take the exam to see what provisions are in place at your school to assist learners with learning challenges.

If the exam date is missed, the only option to make it up may be at the next scheduled administration. Obviously, this only delays the completion of the program and raises stress levels. Do everything possible to take the exam when it is offered. If it is absolutely impossible to take the exam when scheduled, check with your committee chair or department head to see what options are available.

Preparing for the Comprehensive Exam

There are many techniques to consider when preparing for the comprehensive exam. Review class notes, outlines, and old exams, and create a list of major points covered in each course. Take the time to clarify points that you may have missed in the various courses. Don't fail to discuss the comp with your committee. Resist the temptation to cram it all in at the last minute. This generally doesn't work as there is so much to review. A more sensible approach is to plan large blocks of uninterrupted study time. Arrange to discuss areas of concerns with other learners in the student lounge or in the online chat room. Eat and sleep well. Exercise. Let's look at these suggestions in more detail.

Consult with Your Chair and Committee Members

When preparing for the comp, you should discuss any and all concerns with your chair or advisor. Being nervous or apprehensive about the written or oral part is a perfectly normal reaction. The committee chair should recognize this and may have some helpful suggestions.

Ask your chair or individual committee members if they can suggest ways to prepare for the exam. After all, it is virtually impossible to review in detail everything that has been covered in courses over the past several years. Being concerned with time management, you want to make the best use of available time.

What you really desire is to know which questions will be on the exam. Why not come out and discuss this with your chair and committee members? The worst that can happen is to be told nothing. More likely, some direction will be provided.

When seeking direction, listen carefully to what is being said. Don't be guilty of practicing selective hearing. If the committee member tells you there will probably be a question or two on statistics, and statistics is not a strength of yours, wishing it would go away won't help. Careful probing might even help determine what specific statistical techniques will be on the exam.

The same idea applies to any course that has presented problems for you in the past. If it is in your program of study and you have a problem with it, Murphy's Law says that a question related to that course will probably be on the comp. You know what was learned in a course regardless of the grade that was earned. If you haven't done well or are uncertain of what has been learned, it might be wise to audit the class again. Hire a tutor if it will help, but don't think the tutor will teach everything that hasn't been learned before.

Once you have determined potential problem areas, do something to turn this around. Form a study group. Create an online chat group. Meet on a regular basis with a fellow learner. Discuss areas of concern with your professors or committee members and seek their advice about what to do to turn this lemon into lemonade.

Review Course Notes and Textbooks

When preparing for your comp, trying to memorize the text or every note from every course is impossible. It's also an incredible waste of time.

Instead, review class notes and any marginal notes you have written in your textbooks, and summarize the notes into a coherent, logical sequence or pattern. Some people have found writing summaries to be useful, as the physical act of writing reinforces the thinking-and-review process. Some learners write summaries on 3x5 cards. Some use their computer to store summaries on the hard drive and a disc so they won't be lost and are easily retrievable. Learners in online classes often save discussion room postings as another useful review tool. Whatever method you use, make it easy to review this material while riding on the bus, over lunch, or whenever you have free time.

Review Past Comprehensive Examinations

Some graduate schools provide copies of comp questions that have been used in past years for students to use for review and preparation. A typical comp question to an art historian might be: "Compare and contrast Turner's and Canaletto's views on landscape painting. How has each been influenced by the society in which he lived?" A philosophy major might be asked: "Elaborate on the differences and similarities between modern philosophers such as Descartes and Hume and existentialists such as Sartre. How have these schools of thought aided the development of your own philosophy?" A frequently asked comp question of an adult education major is: "Discuss the concept of 'andragogy.' Is it a philosophy or a practice? Analyze your own practice in light of this concept."

The list of comp questions will probably be extensive and overwhelming. There is no realistic way to write out adequate responses to all the questions on the list. No one is expected to do that, and no one should try. This is not the best way to manage your time. These questions are provided to supplement preparation for the comp, not to supplant it. They serve to give an idea of the complexity and scope of past written exams.

A number of graduate programs provide complete copies not only of past questions but also of responses as well. This can be particularly helpful if the writer of the exam is known. Speaking with that person will provide additional insights. Don't make the mistake of memorizing the responses of this person, as there is no guarantee that the same questions will be asked again or that the answers are particularly good. Use the exam copies as an example, nothing more.

When reviewing prior comps, look at both the content and form of the exam. Are there multiple parts to the question? What types of answers are called for? Comparison? Contrasting? Analysis? Synthesis? Integration? Are any general themes or topics discernible?

If your program does not provide past comp questions or exams, it is still possible to get examples. How? Speak with students or alumni who have recently completed the comps. Having gone through the process, they are frequently able to recall questions and discuss the problems they experienced. How did they feel sitting and writing the exam? What was the oral like? What tips or suggestions can they provide?

A word of caution is in order here as well. Keep in mind that individual opinions are being provided. Just because one person found the exam relatively easy does not mean that you also will find it easy. The reverse is also true. People learn and experience things differently.

Having access to past comps isn't always the blessing it may appear to be. Graduate programs that provide access to past comps may expect more from those taking the exam. More depth, precision, and reference to sources are generally expected.

Form Comp Study Groups

A comp study group is a group of graduate students who meet for the purpose of preparing for the comprehensive exam. Study groups are usually more successful when comps are standardized or when they are scheduled at the same time. The most effective study groups are those that have been formed several months before the exam is given because the more time that is available, the better the group will be able to prepare.

Many learners save time by setting up online discussion groups. These accomplish the same thing as an on-campus study group but save you travel time and the need for everyone to meet at the same time. Many online chat groups cost nothing to set up. You might want to start your own oral comprehensive chat group either online or through your student union. Check out http://groups.yahoo.com for more information about how easy it is to set up and manage an online discussion group. Two wonderful resources to connect with other graduate students are the Association for the Support of Graduate Students (www.asgs.org) and the National Association of Graduate-Professional Students (www.nagps.org). Several online discussion groups provide support for grad students in various stages of their programs. For example, H-Grad, (www.h-net.org/~grad), an electronic network for graduate students around the world, provides a safe, student-only forum for discussing issues related to graduate school in humanities-based professions. PhinisheD (http://www.phinished.org) is an international graduate students discussion group seeking to help one another complete their graduate studies. Click on http://gradschoolforum.com and you will be directed to a forum for grad students that invites discussion on everything from admission to dissertation completion.

There is no prescribed format for a study group. Basically, the group looks at how best to prepare for the exam. Sometimes members who are particularly strong or have a particular interest in a subject or course act as tutors or discussion leaders for the rest of the group. They may prepare and deliver a mini-lecture or paper of some sort designed to stimulate thought and group discussion. Another variation is for each group member to prepare a series of questions or concerns on a particular topic for the group to consider. The success of any study group is intimately connected with the amount of support members provide one another. A supportive and nonthreatening environment is a critical part of the success of any support group.

When past comps are available, individual members can assume the task of reviewing them and reporting about both the form and the content of the questions. Group question analysis is often more effective than individual analysis, because when several individuals critique a prior comp question, it is inevitable that several different interpretations or rationales will be identified. This leads to more in-depth comparison, synthesis, integration, and so on.

Some study groups have reviewed past exams to see if certain questions or certain types of questions have appeared more often than others. Others have identified the recurring themes, thoughts, ideas, or references that seem to regularly appear on the comps.

The study group might want to invite students who have recently completed the comps to speak with them. This can be done relatively easily and inexpensively online by using Web-based programs such as Logitech (www.logitech.com), SKYPE (www.skype.com), Windows Live Messenger (http://download.live.com/?sku=messenger), or any program that allows for online meetings. There is nothing more assuring than hearing from fellow students who have passed the exam. In addition to inviting successful graduate students to speak with the group, consider inviting faculty members. They often will provide much different insights.

Groups may wish to set up "mock" exams similar to those that may be in place in your program. This could mean responding in writing to questions either obtained from the graduate program files or prepared by fellow group members. Members of the group could act as the graduate committee at the oral exam. The examinees are expected to respond just as they would at the real thing. Following the exam, the group members offer suggestions to the responder regarding the quality and depth of the responses and provide other constructive criticism about the performance.

Without study groups, preparing for comps can be a lonely and anxious time. Study groups provide support and encouragement to members who are feeling discouraged or who are lacking confidence about the impending exam. Discussing this with someone who is also preparing for comps or who may be experiencing similar emotions may help eliminate the problem or reduce the anxiety. Whatever thoughts or suggestions are offered should be provided in a supportive atmosphere. The study group should not be used to ridicule weaker members or as a platform for the stronger members. The basis of a study group is to help each person recognize weaknesses, strengthen them, and successfully *pass* the comp.

Visit the Test Site

Some grad students worry about the actual test location. Sometimes this drains energy that could be given to reviewing for the exam. A simple suggestion is to visit the test site before the time of the exam. Seeing the site and realizing that it is usually nothing more than a regular classroom, lecture hall, or office can reduce if not eliminate this concern.

Tips for Successfully Completing the Comp Written Exam

Read each question carefully. Outline one or more possible responses. Be sure to include possible references to support response points. Remember to *compare, contrast, analyze, synthesize,* and *integrate.* Weave these concepts into your responses as appropriate. Circle key words. Reword the questions so they are meaningful to you, but be careful not to change the context or intent of the questions. Make sure your responses are clear and unambiguous. Rank the questions from easy to hard, and answer the easier questions first.

The actual act of writing responses to questions over a long period is physically demanding. It is not easy to write continually for several hours at a time. Many individuals find that their fingers begin to cramp from the pressure of holding the pencil or pen. Others experience back or neck pains from sitting in the same position for an extended period.

In Chapter 4, we discussed the relationship between physical condition and program completion. Keeping in good physical shape is also helpful in preparing to take the written comp. A physical conditioning program should be one in which your muscles are stretched and muscle tone is developed.

It should also include practicing relaxation exercises. Those that can be used at any time, such as taking deep breaths and exhaling slowly, are particularly useful. Knowing appropriate relaxation techniques will enable you to apply them as needed when taking the written comp.

Some programs allow a dictionary, pens and pencils, and paper to be brought to the exam. Some will allow the use of books, notes, or whatever tools the student feels are needed to successfully complete the comp. It was not very long ago that calculators were banned from engineering exams. Now they are commonplace.

In this technological age, more and more graduate schools are allowing the use of computers when taking the comp. Others supply everything that is needed and will not allow anything to be brought into the exam room. It is important to know what can be brought into the test site and what is not allowed. Don't make any assumptions about this matter. Instead, ask your chair or department head.

Remember that this is a graduate-level comprehensive exam. It is an opportunity to demonstrate that you have mastered the material in your plan of study and are worthy of receiving a master's or doctoral degree. It also is an opportunity to demonstrate higher-order thinking and writing skills. Sloppy work does not convey the appropriate image. Be sure the responses are more than the reporting back of information gleaned in class. Remember to compare, contrast, analyze, synthesize, and integrate.

Pace yourself. Allow time to review initial responses to the questions. Review the response to determine what may have been omitted. Revise the response accordingly. The time to spot omissions is before the exam is over, not after the exam has been handed in.

The RCOW Process

Let's assume it's the day of the exam. For some time now, you have been preparing for the exam. The waiting has been stressful and has caused a certain degree of anxiety. But now the exam has been distributed and needs to be completed. Time is limited. Do not waste it.

Application of the RCOW (pronounced "are-cow") process can save time and facilitate completion of the exam. RCOW is the process of reading, comprehending, outlining, and writing.

THE RCOW PROCESS

Reading

Comprehending

Outlining

Writing

Begin by *reading* the exam—all of it. Don't write anything yet. Read the directions, each question, everything. Once the entire exam has been read, try to *comprehend* what the questions are about. Think about what is being asked. What course does it relate to? What committee member is interested in this question? Whose concerns are reflected in the question?

At this point, think about which of the questions seems to be the easiest one to answer. Develop an *outline* as a response to this particular question. Include the names or sources of appropriate authors or references to be referred to in the response. Outline the entire response. Think about how much time may be needed to complete this question. Just because it is your strongest response, don't take too long answering it. Remember that all questions need to be answered during the allotted time for the exam.

After the outline is complete, start to *write.* Write in full sentences with correct grammar, punctuation, and syntax. Include an appropriate mix of your thoughts substantiated with references to the research and opinions of the leaders in the field. Be sure to answer all parts of the question. If the question contains multiple parts, as most graduate comp questions do, they are there for a reason and need to be answered. Be sure to provide comparisons if comparisons are asked for. Have you fully compared the landscapes of Turner with Canaletto? Did you remember to respond to the second part of the question?

Once the response to the first question is complete, go on to another. Again, use the RCOW process of reading, comprehending, outlining, and writing. Do this for all the questions, keeping in mind the time allowed to complete the exam.

The RCOW process has helped many graduate students to complete exam questions not only on comps but also on course final exams. Use the process as needed.

The Take-Home Written Exam

Many colleges and universities use a take-home comprehensive exam. This is a situation in which the exam questions are given to you and you are expected to complete them on your own, usually within a prescribed period of time. Just how much time you have depends on your school. Make sure you know how much time you have.

This type of opportunity may sound too good to be true, but a different set of expectations is attached to take-home exams. Granted, the fear of unknown questions is removed. However, the trade-off is that you are expected to produce responses that fully respond to all parts of the question. You have no excuse for omitting comparing and contrasting. There is no excuse for misspelled words or bad grammar. You are expected to produce adequate, sufficient, and relevant references to support each point being made. You won't be forgiven if your responses don't have subheads, with each containing an introduction, appropriately presented and developed points, and followed by conclusions that synthesize or integrate the subsection into a greater whole.

On the plus side, you do have time to think about the questions and develop complete and full responses, go to the library, search the Web, and outline your responses. You can revise as much as you want. You can discuss ideas with other learners. The time pressure is off. This is often a much more satisfying and rewarding way to demonstrate mastery of your program.

The tips for taking the comp written exam are equally appropriate when faced with a take-home exam. Use them!

Tips for Successfully Completing the Comp Oral Exam

For many learners, the oral portion is the most stressful part of the comps, because almost everyone has a certain amount of fear when speaking in front of a group. This fear is greater when the group is your graduate committee, which is charged with the power to determine whether or not you receive the degree. Most learners enter this part of the exam feeling tense and anxious, regardless of how much time has been spent reviewing notes and speaking with committee members or fellow graduate students.

As mentioned earlier in this chapter, not all master's degree programs have an oral exam. It is much more common in doctoral programs. If your program has an oral, here are some suggestions for preparing for and taking this part of the exam.

TIPS FOR SUCCESSFULLY COMPLETING THE ORAL EXAM

1. Be prepared.
2. Use the "count to three" technique.
3. Paraphrase.
4. Be honest.
5. Listen carefully.

Be Prepared

Much of the fear associated with the oral exam concerns perceived rather than real issues. There are all sorts of rumors and horror stories about committee members who get their kicks out of making graduate students squirm. Although some really do enjoy this arrogant display of power, most committee members do not. Most are supportive rather than adversarial, but don't assume that this is always the case. You can control the situation as much as possible by being prepared, composed, and ready.

One way to prepare is to think of this time as a meeting of equals. The committee may have more knowledge and experience, but you have just spent a great deal of time preparing for the comps and should be well prepared and well able to fully discuss the relevant theories, authorities, experts, and concepts of the field, particularly as they relate to the written comp.

The "Count to Three" Technique

A good way to maintain control at this difficult time is to use the "count to three" technique before speaking. This simply means mentally counting to three before responding. The technique is a subtle but effective control device because it gives the impression that you are thinking before responding and that the answer may have some basis in the literature. Whether this is true or not is not important. The impression it gives is the main point. Mentally counting to three before responding gives the impression of being in control. It also provides "think time" to develop an answer. It is surprising how much the mind can come up with, given those three extra seconds to work.

All too often, especially in times of stress, graduate students are so nervous that they jump in with a response before the question being asked has been fully developed. This can be devastating, particularly if the question being asked is not the question you answer. Using the "count to three" technique before responding helps to avoid this pitfall.

Paraphrase

Another strategy is to paraphrase the question before answering. This is based on the idea that people communicate in many different styles. For example, when some people begin to speak, they are not exactly sure of the point they want to make and begin with seemingly vague or unconnected statements. Their question or point is usually made clearer in their last few sentences. Others make their point at the beginning of their statement and then go on to elaborate. Frequently, the elaboration is unclear or unnecessary and leads the listener to believe that another, different point is being made. The intent of the speaker to clarify the point or question through elaboration may not be understood by the listener. The result is that the listener (the graduate student at the oral) doesn't know what point or question is really being asked.

To make matters worse, people usually respond to questions the same way they speak. If one's speaking pattern is to make the point and then to elaborate, the response pattern will probably be to respond to the first part of the speaker's statement. If one's speaking pattern is to make the point at the end of the statement, the response pattern probably will be the same. There is not much of a problem if the speaker (the committee member) speaks in a manner that corresponds to your response style. Real problems can occur at the oral when the speaker speaks in a manner different from your preferred response pattern. What can happen is that full communication does not take place; the student is not sure what is being asked but needs to respond. By paraphrasing the question before responding, the examinee is better able to maintain control of the situation, create more "think time" to develop a response, and importantly, avoid answering the wrong question.

Paraphrasing is a very simple technique. In your own words, simply restate the question being asked. Examples of paraphrasing are these: "In other words, are you asking me to compare Descartes with Hume rather than to discuss Descartes?" or "I'm not exactly certain what you are asking but I think you wanted me to not only discuss 'andragogy' but also to analyze my own office based on this concept. Is this what you want me to do?" The questioner will either agree and give you the opportunity to answer or disagree and more clearly articulate the question or point. Either way, you have bought time to formulate a more thoughtful response.

Be Honest

During the oral, it is important to be honest about what you know and what you don't know. Realize that there might well be several questions to which the answers are unknown to you. This is not unusual. Don't try to bluff the committee. This only serves to challenge them, and they will usually come out the winner. A better approach would be to admit the uncertainty and demonstrate an awareness of how to obtain the answer by referring to appropriate sources or references for the answer. Another honest approach would be to pick a subsection of the answer that is known and focus on that.

Listen Carefully

Listen carefully to what is being asked at the oral. Some helpful tips are:

1. Eliminate distractions. Look directly at the speaker.
2. Control your emotions. Avoid prejudging and listen without interrupting.

3. Occasionally take notes. Writing it down helps you to concentrate on the question being asked.
4. Listen actively. Nod, smile; let your eyes show surprise, interest, delight, or concern.

Practice these techniques. For example, the next time a friend asks a question, make a conscious effort to look directly into his or her eyes the entire time the question is being asked. Nod appropriately. Try not to interrupt. After you have given your response and the conversation is concluded, ask your friend for any reaction regarding your nonverbal action. How did your friend feel when you were looking directly into his or her eyes? What image did it project? Was there any reaction to the nodding of your head and not interrupting? How did you feel about this?

Take notes the next time you are being asked a question. Explain that this is being done as an aid to providing a full response. When the question-and-answer period is over, ask the person or group for reactions. Did they feel respected? Neglected? Did they feel you were sincerely interested in them? How did you feel? Did it give you time to think about a response? Did it help you to give a more accurate response?

As with any new technique, try it and determine how it works for you. The more these techniques are used, the more natural they will become.

7

PROPOSAL AND THE THESIS/ DISSERTATION

> About a year into my graduate program I remember coming home one night and telling my wife that I was dropping out. How could I be expected to complete the thesis with everything else going on in my life?
>
> Her response was perfect. She listened, sympathized, and encouraged me to talk about the problem. Later that week, I made an appointment with my chairperson and discussed it with him. I learned I wasn't alone. It is not easy to complete something as meaningful as a graduate degree.
>
> —*Ted*

The culminating experience in most graduate programs generally is referred to as a *thesis* at the master's level and a *dissertation* at the doctoral level. Some programs, particularly at the master's level, call it a *final project.* The *proposal* is a description of what the thesis, dissertation, or final project will contain.

Many, but not all, master's programs require a thesis. In those master's programs not requiring a thesis, a comprehensive examination is often the culminating degree experience. As mentioned in Chapter 6, the comps are frequently called the "prelims" or "qualifying exam." The comps usually serve to integrate the information that has been imparted in the various courses. Almost every doctoral program requires a dissertation or its equivalent. It is difficult to settle on one word to describe the dissertation or its equivalent, because some doctoral programs refer to it as a thesis and some master's programs call it a dissertation. Some graduate programs add to the confusion by calling it a research project or an applied research project, regardless of whether it is at the master's or the doctoral level. There should be no difference in the quality or the development of a thesis or dissertation produced in an accredited campus-based or distance-education graduate program. However, just as the reputations of all campus-based programs are not the same and don't have identical expectations, the same is also true of distance-education graduate programs.

Each graduate program has its own policies and procedures for developing the proposal and completing the study or project. In the development of the proposal, most faculty are more concerned with the quality of the work than the number of pages. They will check to see if you have completely described the problem or topic, reviewed the literature as it relates to the topic, and presented appropriate methodology.

Several books are available to assist with the development of the proposal and/or the thesis/dissertation. The references at the end of this book list several of these resources. The books listed under "Guides to Writing a Proposal, Thesis, Dissertation, or Research Paper" provide very helpful generic information. Another section in the reference list is "Research and Writing in the Disciplines." The information in this section provides more specific information relative to what is needed in the various disciplines. Most of these sources suggest that there is a general pattern to follow when developing the proposal, and that it is vital to be aware of this pattern as well as the requirements established by your graduate program.

As has been suggested throughout this book, it is very important to know and follow program policies and procedures and to know the concerns of your advisor and committee. It is just as important to maintain as much control over the development of both the form and content of the proposal and the completed study as it is for any other part of the graduate program.

Before writing anything, however, be sure to become familiar with the formal and informal procedures and processes in place in your program. Talk with current and former students, program administrators, and faculty. Review copies of completed proposals, theses, and dissertations on file in the main university or college library or in the department.

ProQuest UMI Dissertation Publishing

No discussion about the proposal and dissertation would be complete without the mention of ProQuest UMI Dissertation Publishing, one of the world's largest and most widely used bibliographic information files. The ProQuest UMI Dissertation Services program maintains the definitive bibliographic record for more than 2.3 million doctoral dissertations and master's theses published worldwide. More than 70,000 new works are published each year from graduates of the more than 700 colleges and university ProQuest partners. The database includes citations for materials ranging from the first U.S. dissertation, accepted in 1861, to those accepted as recently as last semester.

Most graduate school libraries maintain the ProQuest UMI Dissertation database. As a graduate student, you will be able to search the database and gain access to invaluable research related to your dissertation or thesis topic. Once you find the appropriate dissertations or theses, they can be purchased for a modest fee.

In 2008, UMI Dissertation Publishing launched "Open Access Publishing," a term used to describe content that can be accessed free of charge. Through Open Access, students can access many dissertations and thesis at no cost.

More information can be obtained from ProQuest UMI Dissertation Publishing, 789 E. Eisenhower Parkway, P.O. Box 1346, Ann Arbor, MI. 48106-1346, www.proquest.com/en-US/products/dissertations.

The Pre-Proposal

Many graduate programs require the submission of a *pre-proposal* (sometimes called a *précis*) before permission is granted to develop the full proposal. Essentially, the pre-proposal is a shortened form or outline of the proposal. Its purpose is to help with the development of the proposed topic or concept, identification of appropriate literature, and review of possible methodologies and/or data analysis techniques. For more details regarding the components of the proposal, see the section "Connecting the Proposal to the Thesis/Dissertation" later in this chapter.

A pre-proposal should fit on one page. The example on the following page is provided as a guide.

Feel free to develop a pre-proposal for every idea you feel may be appropriate as a possible topic. If a thesis or dissertation is a required component of your program, you should begin thinking of possible topics as soon as you enter the program and develop a pre-proposal for every possible topic or variation thereof. This also helps you to understand how the dissertation may interact with, evolve from, and/or relate to issues or concerns raised in class, course reading or projects, comp questions, the work environment, or other "real-life" problems.

Try very hard to keep the pre-proposal to one page. When you are confined to a one-page form, you are forced to be concise and succinct.

Prior to meeting with your major advisor, you will have developed not only several possible problem areas but also possible problem statements and objectives of the study. For each possible topic, you will have also considered relative importance of the study, topics in the literature that could possibly constitute the theoretical framework of the study, possible ways of responding to the problem, and a short working title of the study.

THE PRE-PROPOSAL

Statement of the Problem:

Objectives of the Study:

Importance or Significance of the Study:

Topics of the Literature to Be Reviewed:

Proposed Methodology:

Proposed Title (in 12 words or fewer):

How to Develop the Pre-Proposal

Make multiple copies of the pre-proposal form. Complete the form as completely as you can any time a possible thesis or dissertation topic presents itself. For example, let's assume that you are a classroom teacher and are concerned with charter schools. Perhaps an article in the newspaper or a report on the evening news has raised questions about the effectiveness of charter schools. Rather than take personal offense and complain that "they don't know what they are talking about," a better idea might be to think of the effectiveness of charter schools as a possible topic for your study. Can this be developed into a problem statement? What specific objectives about charter schools might be studied? Why is this important? What possible literature topics (not specific studies) might form the theoretical framework within which charter schools could be studied? What are some possible ways the problem could be studied (i.e., interviews with students, parents, teachers, school administrators? Analyses of data within the school? Comparing data from several charter schools?)? What could be the title of the study ("A Comparative Analysis of the Effectiveness of Charter Schools in XXX County")? Thus, a pre-proposal form has just been developed.

Another topic could evolve from discussion in class. Let's assume you are a business manager in a class on leadership. The "situational leadership" theory promulgated by Ken Blanchard and others is being discussed. You realize that your style is predominantly that of a "directing" leader and that you are not able to effectively change leadership styles to adapt to the changing situation. You might begin to wonder, "What would happen to my department if I was able to change my leadership style as needed?" Is this a possible dissertation topic? Look at the pre-proposal form. What is the specific problem or topic to be considered? What is the statement of the problem? What are the specific objectives to be studied related to this problem? Why is it important? How does this fit in with existing knowledge? How could this problem be studied? What is the specific title of this study?

The Statement of the Problem

This should be no more than 3–5 sentences. The statement of the problem should be something that is personally challenging and serves as a tool for planning and guiding the research that is to come. It should reflect a lack of information or knowledge, the presence of which would help alleviate the problem. It should not be something that is readily answered by a review of existing knowledge or research, nor should it have been already solved elsewhere by someone else.

Objectives of the Study

An *objective* is a clear and unambiguous description of an expectation related to the central problem or topic of the study. It could include an examination of certain behaviors, the conditions of performance to be assessed, or establishing certain minimum performance criteria.

Objectives of the study could relate to the discovery of specific knowledge, understanding of meaning, application (i.e., how specific information or theories were used to solve specific problems), analysis (i.e., the breaking down of informational materials into their component parts), synthesis (i.e., how application of prior knowledge and skills produce a new or original whole), or evaluation (i.e., the rendering of a judgment resulting in an end product, with a given purpose, without real right or wrong answers).

Consider three to five objectives for the study. Less is too few, and more than five are usually too ambitious.

Importance or Significance of the Study

This section of the pre-proposal discusses why the study is being conducted. Why is it important? To whom is it important? How will the results of the study affect the learner's operation? What about similar programs in other parts of the state, region, or country? If several different perspectives can't be presented, a very basic question must be asked of the researcher: Why is this study being considered, or what will this add to the knowledge base?

Topics of the Literature to be Reviewed

This relates to the literature review that forms chapter 2 of the dissertation. Briefly, the purpose of the literature review is to provide the context within which the study will be developed and framed. In the pre-proposal, consider the topics (not specific studies) that may help establish the context in which the study will eventually be placed.

Consider the following questions when developing this section:

1. What topics in the literature might shed light on the history of the problem?
2. What topics in the literature might provide a theoretical background to the problem?
3. What topics in the literature might justify the importance or significance of the problem?
4. What topics in the literature might justify the selection of a particular method to respond to the problem?

Proposed Methodology

This section of the pre-proposal is *not* intended to provide a detailed description of the research methodology. This will be developed much more fully in the proposal and will be included as chapter 3 of the dissertation. The purpose of this section in the pre-proposal is to encourage the student to think about the techniques that will be used to respond to the objectives. For example, will certain populations be interviewed? Will an experimental design be used? Will programs be compared? Will a combination of techniques be used?

Proposed Title in Twelve Words or Fewer

I have purposely placed this section at the end of the form and urge students *not* to think of a title until after they have completed the other parts of the form. I have found that if students think about the general nature of the problem, the objectives, the significance, literature topics, and methodology *before* trying to develop a title, they won't waste too much time trying to create a title of the study. If they develop the title *after* they have completed the other elements, they will more easily develop the title as they have already given considerable thought to the study and the various component parts. As a result, the title more easily flows.

I am quite serious about the title consisting of twelve words or fewer. My experience with developing a title for the study indicates that when students are limited to twelve words, they think more about a title that adequately describes the study and does so in a way that is easily understood by all.

Even if a pre-proposal is not required by your college or university, it is a good idea to develop one; doing so encourages refinement of often vague ideas relating to the various parts of the proposed study(s). It also provides an opportunity to interact with the committee. By developing a pre-proposal, you have a tangible way of obtaining committee feedback prior to spending time and effort developing the proposal. It also encourages you to think about how the topic you are interested in lends itself to a graduate study. Unfortunately, some worthy problem areas, though important in and of themselves, are simply too broad, nebulous, or ambiguous to be considered as a dissertation.

A major advantage of the pre-proposal is that it serves to facilitate discussion of possible thesis/dissertation study topics without the need for the student to develop a fully developed proposal. The judicious use of the one-page pre-proposal will save the student valuable time and effort as it opens discussion on a variety of possible topics with relatively little time being spent to more fully develop these topics.

Developing the Proposal

Sharan Merriam and Edwin Simpson's book, *A Guide to Research for Educators and Trainers of Adults* (2000), provides a very helpful outline that can be used as a guide for both the proposal and the first three chapters of the final report. The outline that follows will be discussed in more detail later in this chapter.

A. Introduction and Problem (chapter 1 of the study)
    - Introduction to the study
    - Background to the study
    - Statement of the problem (what is the problem or area of concern?)
    - Purpose of the study (specific purposes and/or objectives)
    - Rationale or theoretical basis for the study
    - Hypotheses or questions to be answered
    - Importance or significance of the study
    - Definition of terms (operational definitions)
    - Assumptions and limitations of the study
    - Organization of the remainder of the study

B. Review of the Literature (chapter 2)
    - Introduction and organizational structure of the chapter

Abbreviated review of pertinent literature, grouped around major topics or themes

C. Methodology (chapter 3)
   Introduction (reviewing the purpose of the study)
   Description of methodology to be used (e.g., experimental, case study, historical)
   Design of the study (operationalization of variables)
   Sample and population or source of data
   Instrumentation
   Data collection and other procedures
   Data analysis (how do you expect to analyze the data once they are collected?)

Some graduate programs have an unstructured process for the development of the proposal. This is to provide maximum flexibility and creativity and not to let form restrict the free flow of ideas. In these programs, students are encouraged to develop the topic, discuss and negotiate it with their chair and their committee, and refine it as needed.

In many other programs, a carefully structured process is in place regarding the development of the proposal. Guidelines and manuals are provided, and you are expected to strictly adhere to them when developing your proposal.

Ultimately, the proposal is approved by the committee and/or the graduate program and provides a skeletal understanding of what will be completed for the thesis or dissertation. It is not uncommon for the proposal to be fully developed into three chapters, which will essentially be the first three chapters of the thesis or dissertation.

The Thesis/Dissertation

Although the names of the chapters may vary, the most common outline for a thesis or dissertation is the following five-chapter format:

Chapter 1: The Problem or Topic
Chapter 2: The Literature Review
Chapter 3: The Methodology
Chapter 4: Presentation and Analysis of the Data
Chapter 5: Summary, Conclusions, and Recommendations

The first chapter basically describes the problem or topic. A variety of subsections within chapter 1 develop the topic more fully and describe it in considerable detail. The second chapter contains a complete review of the literature that is directly and indirectly related to the problem or topic just described in chapter 1. It provides the context and theoretical framework for the problem or topic (e.g., how it relates to other literature in the field). The third chapter is a complete description of the methodology that will be used to respond to the problem. The fourth chapter contains the data that have been collected using the methodology described in chapter 3. The fifth chapter completes the study by presenting conclusions and recommendations based on the data presented in chapter 4.

Connecting the Proposal to the Thesis/Dissertation

It is helpful to think of the proposal in relation to the first three chapters of the completed study. Indeed, many graduate programs require that the proposal contain these three chapters. The proposal is a description of something to be done in the future; therefore, the proposal is written in the *future tense.* The final thesis or dissertation describes the completed project and is always written in the *past tense.* Thus, it is not unusual that with tense changes from future to past and other modifications, the proposal will essentially become the first three chapters of the final study.

The purpose of the proposal is to describe in some detail the topic or problem, the literature related to the topic, and the methodology selected to respond to the topic. The topic is described in chapter 1 of the proposal. Literature relevant to the topic is presented in chapter 2, and the appropriate methodology is presented in chapter 3.

Think of the proposal and the thesis/dissertation as analogous to a blueprint and the building of a house. The blueprint presents a skeletal picture of the house and provides a fairly good idea of what it will look like when it is built. The blueprint encourages conferences with others and conceptual changes to be made prior to actually beginning the construction. So it is with the proposal. The proposal allows for the conceptualization of the topic, organization of the literature around the main ideas of the topic, and a discussion of the proposed methodology *prior* to conducting the study.

Chapter 1: The Problem

Chapter 1 of the proposal and the completed study are pretty much the same. Both fully describe the study problem or topic using subheadings similar to those indicated earlier. This can usually be done in about 10–12 double-spaced pages.

Introduction and Background

The introduction and background sections provide the reader with an overview of the topic or problem. It should be fairly brief (two to three pages), yet complete enough to give the reader a clear idea of the topic or idea. It should include a sufficient number of major references but not everything that has been written related to the topic. The bulk of the literature review is presented in chapter 2. These sections are intended to introduce the reader to the topic and should not be overwhelming.

For example, let's assume you are interested in the general topic of child care in industry. After thinking about this topic and talking about it with friends, colleagues, and family, you develop a one-page pre-proposal concerned with this general topic. After a discussion of the pre-proposal with your major advisor and committee, you decide that the focus of your study is to determine whether child-care needs in your company (the XYZ Corporation) are perceived differently by labor and management.

In the introduction section of chapter 1, it is entirely appropriate to introduce the reader to the topic by discussing how the family has changed in the past two or three generations and how this has affected business. You would cite major authorities who have written on this subject or relevant statistical data to support the idea that effective child-care programs have affected business and industry. After a page or two of this type of general introductory material, the reader should have a sense of the general nature of the problem of the study.

Next, more definite background information regarding child care as it relates to industry is provided. Two or three sources supporting specific or major themes or ideas regarding child care and industry are in order. Again, this section is not intended to be all-inclusive, but it should show that this is a topic worthy of further investigation or research.

Statement of the Problem

Follow your overview with a very brief (one- to two-paragraph) section referred to as the Statement of the Problem. This is a succinct summation of the topic of the study. It should end with a completion of the following sentence: "Therefore, the topic (or problem) of this study is. . . ." The latter part of this sentence should clearly reflect the twelve-word title of the study that was suggested in the pre-proposal. By ending with this sentence, the reader should now have a clear and unambiguous understanding of the problem or topic of the study.

Continuing with the child-care example, once the introductory and general background information have been provided, the Statement of the Problem section might end with this sentence: "Therefore, the topic of this study are perceptual differences of labor and management regarding child-care needs of XYZ Corporation."

Purpose or Objectives

Now that the topic has been introduced, background information provided, and problem succinctly stated, the proposal needs to describe the purpose(s) and/or objective(s) as they relate to the statement of the problem. This is provided in the Purpose of the Study section. What part or parts of the topic are of specific interest?

This section also is fairly brief (one to two pages) and clearly articulates the specific objectives or purposes of the study. This also serves to further focus the study. Objectives and purposes can be presented as a list or in narrative fashion.

An example for the XYZ Corporation follows.

The specific objectives of this study are:

1. to determine the child-care needs of XYZ Corporation as perceived by labor,
2. to determine the child-care needs of XYZ Corporation as perceived by management,
3. to compare differences in perceptions by labor and management regarding the child-care needs of the XYZ Corporation.

Theoretical or Conceptual Framework

Next, the rationale or theoretical basis for the study is presented. This section may also be referred to as the Theoretical or Conceptual Framework. Its purpose is to develop and present an understanding of how the problem relates to a unified explanation of related ideas and to provide the foundation on which the study will build and develop. This section further expounds on the topic by providing a summary of the major theories or research supporting, clarifying, refuting, or driving the notion that perceptions of labor and management may differ or may be perceived differently. It may also include references to similar studies in related areas and provide a rationale that labor and management will frequently have differing perceptions of a variety of topics. These topics or themes are elaborated on more fully in chapter 2.

The theoretical framework is one of the most difficult sections to develop, because it depends on an awareness of the value of theory in research. As it is almost impossible to clearly define theory, it is clear why this section is so hard to develop, let alone get faculty agreement on its relationship to your study.

When developing this section, remember that the place of theory in the study depends on what is known about the particular topic. When dealing with the general topic of motivation, for example, much available research has been synthesized, directed, or guided by theory. However, much less research has been conducted on adult motivation. Therefore, there are many fewer theories to connect with the topic of adult motivation. The researcher's task is to decide, and ultimately to get the committee to agree, that the study is testing a well-developed theory; clarifying, refining, or adding to a tentative theory; or seeking to develop a new theory.

When looking at the place of theory in our illustrative child-care example, this section would review theories relating to needs assessment and differences in perception and provide a rationale for how they relate to the topic.

Hypotheses or Research Questions to Be Answered

The "Hypotheses" or "Questions to Be Answered" section is the next stage in the process of identifying, defining, and clarifying the problem. Whether the study will have hypotheses or questions to be answered depends on the type of study being conducted. Broadly stated, research questions guide past- and present-oriented, descriptive, comparative, and/or evaluative studies such as case studies, historical studies, and simple correlational studies. Hypotheses are used in future-oriented, quantitative studies such as single- or multiple-group experiments.

Research questions are posed when one is working in areas that are relatively new or in which a great deal of prior research has not been conducted. Research questions serve to guide the research and provide an outline for presenting the data. When working in areas in which significant research has been done, it is more likely that hypotheses will be included, as a hypothesis provides greater precision and predictive power. Similar to research questions, hypotheses also serve to provide a basic outline for presenting the data.

It is common for a research study to contain both questions and hypotheses. Again, this will depend on the topic of the study and the amount of research that has already been done. In our child-care example, one hypothesis with several parts would probably be used, because a great deal of research has been done and theories produced in the areas of child-care needs and perceptual differences related to needs. For this example, the hypothesis might be as follows:

There are no significant differences in the child-care needs of XYZ Corporation as perceived by labor and management.

Importance or Significance of the Study

This section probes why the study is being conducted. Why is it important? To whom is it important? How will the results of the study affect not only the XYZ Corporation but also other local corporations with child-care programs? What about other corporations in other parts of the state, region, or country? If several different perspectives can't be presented, again, a very basic question must be asked of the researcher: Why is this study being considered and what will this add to knowledge base?

Definition of Terms

Within this section, operational definitions of major words or terms used in the study are provided. This section is included to aid the reader in understanding how specific terms are being used in the study. Common, generally accepted terms associated with child-care programs in industry or with the research methodology being proposed are not routinely defined. Only uncommon terms or common ones being used in uncommon, unusual, or unconventional ways need to be defined.

For example, the child-care program in the XYZ Corporation may be set up for "latchkey" children. As there is no commonly accepted definition for *latchkey,* this term needs to be defined as used in the study.

If one decides to use a variation of an accepted research methodology, this would be defined as well. Keep in mind, however, that some faculty prefer that anything related to the methodology be included in the methodology chapter. As always, fully discuss and negotiate any concerns with your chair or advisor and committee members.

Words or terms needing definitions are often found in the title of the study and in the purposes, objectives, rationale, hypotheses, and research questions sections. They should be briefly defined in chapter 1 and may be elaborated on in the literature review section in chapter 2.

In the XYZ Corporation example, *at least* the following terms should be defined:

XYZ Corporation
Child-care program in XYZ Corporation
Labor
Management
Perception

Assumptions and Limitations

The purpose of the "Assumptions and Limitations" section of the proposal is difficult to clearly discuss because there is no general consensus regarding its function or what needs to be included. As always, once you have determined the assumptions and limitations appropriate to your study, discuss and negotiate them with your committee chair and committee members and come to an agreement regarding how this section relates to the study and what needs to be included.

Generally speaking, a section discussing the major assumptions underlying the study is required by most graduate schools. The researcher, in conjunction with the committee, needs to determine what is a major assumption and what is not.

Many different types of assumptions may relate to the population or sample used in the study, or they may be concerned with subtle differences regarding cultures or societies. They may relate to age, sex, or other demographic variables among the study population. Assumptions may relate to the measures or to other aspects of the research design and methodology (e.g., is it assumed that the personality test developed for the study is valid and adequately measures the personality characteristics that are central to the study?). Make the initial decisions about the importance of the assumptions and whether they need to be included in this section in consultation with your advisor.

Limitations provide another way to further clarify, quantify, delimit, or define certain aspects of the problem or topic that cannot easily be included in any of the sections discussed so far. The intent of the limitations section is to give special emphasis or to further clarify limiting factors that could not have been avoided or corrected for in the study, such as the honesty or truthfulness of the respondents or unanticipated variables in the pilot study that were impossible to predict or control. It also provides the researcher with an opportunity to anticipate problems in the proposal and to describe them in the dissertation.

Some programs add to the confusion by using *delimitations.* This is usually a planned limitation due to the lack of time or resources (e.g., the study could be implemented only during the fall semester, or funds to train interviewers were only available for a specific three-week period).

Let's take another look at the child-care program of the XYZ Corporation. In this program, let's say the "latchkey" kids make up 85 percent of the children in the program. Although this may have been discussed in earlier sections of chapter 1, it should be mentioned in this section as a limitation because it possibly affects the generalizability or application of your results to other child-care programs in similar companies.

Organization of the Remainder of the Study

The purpose of this section is to tell the reader what to expect in the remaining chapters. This alerts the reader to any deviation from that which is traditionally included in the remaining chapters. This section could be a paragraph such as the following:

Chapter 2 will discuss the appropriate literature related to the problem just described. Chapter 3 will describe and discuss the research methodology selected to respond to the problem. Chapter 4 will present and analyze the data collected using the methodology described in Chapter 3. The study will conclude with Chapter 5, which is a brief summary of Chapters 1–4, conclusions drawn from the data presented in Chapter 4, and recommendations for future research.

Chapter 2: The Literature Review

Chapter 2 of the proposal and the thesis/dissertation is the literature review. In the proposal, it is frequently a brief review of pertinent literature grouped by major themes or topics. Some graduate programs require that it be completely developed in the proposal. Others may require an abbreviated review for the proposal and expect that the fully developed review will be in place in the final document.

The literature review includes books, articles, interviews, and other print or nonprint sources of opinion, fact, or empirical data that provide a context for your study. It can also include relevant Web pages or other Web-related material. The purpose of the literature review is to demonstrate that you are as current as anyone about what has been done related to the topic. A well-done literature review can establish you as an expert. At the very least, it should reveal that you know a lot about your topic and have a good working knowledge of directly and indirectly related literature.

It is impossible to prescribe how many pages are appropriate for this chapter. This is determined by the topics and themes directly and indirectly related to the problem. It is not unusual for a completely developed chapter 2 to contain fifty to seventy-five pages.

In today's electronic world, it is easy to find sources. However, all sources are not equal. Primary sources or references (i.e., firsthand testimony or direct evidence concerning a topic under investigation usually created by those who experienced the events or conditions being documented) are always preferable to secondary sources (sources that may cite, comment, or build on primary sources). In the natural and social sciences, the results of an experiment or study published as an article in a refereed journal or papers discussing findings that are delivered at conferences are considered primary sources. When a primary source is not available, a secondary source might work. It is critical that all sources, including those with Web addresses, are correctly cited in your work.

A word of caution needs to be added when using the Internet to search for relevant literature. There are no restrictions regarding what can be placed on the Internet. Unlike refereed journals or books from reputable publishers, anyone can post anything on the Internet with little or no safeguards concerning its accuracy or authenticity. It becomes imperative that grad students be even more astute and critical when including material discovered on the Internet as part of the literature review.

ACTS—Guidelines for Assessing Literature

ACTS is a process for assessing the relevance of literature to one's proposal or dissertation. It is appropriate when assessing literature located online or through more traditional sources. When using the ACTS approach, the learner should review material from four perspectives. Is the material authoritative? Is it current? Is it truthful? Is it supported? Let's look more closely at these perspectives.

ACTS

Is the literature **A**uthoritative?

Is the literature **C**urrent and **C**orrect?

Is the literature **T**ruthful?

Is the literature **S**upported

Authoritative. This suggests that the reader consider the trustworthiness of the piece. Who wrote it? How well known is the author? What type of organizational support is provided to the author? What else has been written or produced by the author? What quality control standards are evident (i.e., has the article been subjected to a peer review)?

Current and Correct. This suggests that the reader should look at when the article was written and should also try to determine the correctness of the material. In what year was it written? What are facts and what are opinions? Is it timely? Is it complete? What is the intended audience? Whose voices are being reflected?

Truthful. This means looking at the reasonableness of the piece. Is it fair? Does it reflect differing perspectives? Is it objective? Does it present the opinions and findings of others? Is it presented in as unbiased a manner as possible? Is the author connected with an industry, political party, or interest group that might benefit from the publication of this piece?

Supportable. The piece should be supported by data or it should clearly indicate that it is the opinion or viewpoint of the author. The reviewer of the piece should determine as well as possible if the material is supported by references. Who has written the references? Is there more than one reference in support of each statement of fact? Are all claims supported? Is there consistency among the sources?

Purposes of the Literature Review

There are at least five major purposes of the literature:

1. To place the topic in a historical context
2. To provide for the assessment of previous studies
3. To justify selection of the topic
4. To assist in the selection of the research design and methodological procedures
5. To provide the theoretical framework

Establishing the Historical Context. It is fairly safe to say that no topic exists in isolation. When faced with making sense out of reams of computer-generated abstracts of literature relating to the topic, you may wish this were true, but it isn't. When writing about the topic, the need is to establish where it fits in relation to current and past studies. What aspects of the problem have been studied? When were the studies completed? What problems have been encountered? How have they been resolved? Looking at the historical context will also help to establish how your study is different from other studies and help to establish researcher credibility.

Assessing Previous Studies. The literature review also provides an assessment of previous studies as they relate to the topic. How reliable are the data and the analysis? How sound are the recommendations? How and why is the cited literature relevant to your topic?

Using the "Five Ws" to Assess Relevant Literature. The five Ws (who, what, where, when, and why) are helpful in determining the literature to be included or omitted. When looking at the "who" aspect, consider the reputation of the author. How well known is this person? How many books, chapters, articles, and so on has this person published? How prestigious are the journals or publishers that publish this person's work? With the computer capabilities of most research libraries, it is relatively easy to run a search of the appropriate databases and determine how often the author and the articles have been cited. Another dimension of "who" is to consider the population constituting the focus of the research. How was the population sampled, and what was the extent of the sampling? How does the "who" of this literature relate to your study?

Assess the literature in terms of "what" has been done as well as "what" are the results of that research. How can you use this literature? How does this relate to the proposed topic?

When looking at "where," most literature reflects at least one of the following four perspectives: local, regional, national, and international. Review the literature from the most relevant perspective(s). For example, when considering a topic relating to industrial psychology, looking at regional differences might be considered irrelevant, as people learn through the same basic psychological processes in California as they do in New York. However, if the study is concerned with differences in attitudes, it is impossible to assume that the opinions of individuals in the West are the same as those in the East. The key to controlling this is to know the topic and to review the literature accordingly. The same logic can be applied to reviewing literature with a local, national, or international flavor.

The purpose of reviewing literature from a "when" perspective is to determine the currency of the material. Research often runs in cycles. There are times when a great deal of research is done on a particular subject, interest subsides, and then, for no apparent reason, it picks up again. Be sure to know if the literature being reviewed is in an up or down cycle.

There are several other reasons for needing to know when the research was done. It will help establish the historical basis for the research. It will determine if the research interest in this topic has waned. If this is so, the following question is a good one to ask: "Why am I interested in it?" Knowing when the study was done will also help determine if replicability is needed or warranted. Would a study completed in 1950 have the same results if completed on a similar population today?

Justification of the Topic. The last of the five *W*s ("why") helps not only to assess literature but also with the third purpose for doing a literature review—to justify the selection of the topic. Why was the study done? What problem was the researcher looking at? How does this problem relate to your study?

Aid in the Selection of Research Design. The fourth purpose of the literature review is to aid in the selection of the research design and methodological procedures. Reviewing the literature to determine what approaches have been used before, as well as their successes and failures, can save a great deal of time, effort, and money. Familiarity with other procedures can provide a base from which the researcher can select, modify, and create new designs useful in developing the proposal or study. Fortunate, indeed, would be the researcher of the XYZ Corporation study who locates a research design or an evaluation instrument that parallels the study with the XYZ Corporation.

A word of caution is necessary here. Check to see if the material is copyrighted. If the questionnaire or instrument is copyrighted, permission from the copyright holder is needed prior to using it. This may involve the payment of a fee. In many cases, the copyright holder will grant permission to use the instrument free of charge. This is particularly true when the material is from a recently completed thesis or dissertation. Fellow students are quick to realize what others are going through and are thrilled and flattered that someone thinks enough of their work to ask permission to use it.

Generally, permission to use a research design is not needed because it is unlikely that every aspect of the copyrighted study will be exactly duplicated. More than likely, some or all of the variables will be changed. The copyright only prevents exact duplication.

If unsure whether to ask permission of the copyright holder, a good rule is to act on the side of caution and ask permission. Check this with your chair as well.

The Theoretical Framework. The fifth purpose of the literature review relates to the theoretical framework, which was discussed earlier in this chapter. Within the literature review chapter of the proposal, the material may have been summarized or briefly presented. In the final report, the literature review provides a strong theoretical framework for the study. For example, how do the different theories regarding perception relate to the XYZ Corporation? On what basis were certain theories rejected as being irrelevant? In this section, the reader is provided with an increased understanding of the theoretical underpinnings as they relate to the study. In other words, what theory or theories are driving the study? How will they provide the basis for interpreting the data and presenting the implications of the findings?

A literature review that is logically organized, places the topic in a historical context, and presents a critical examination of the strengths and weaknesses of related research designs, methodologies, and theories of related studies will strengthen the claim that the topic is important and worthy of a research study at the master's or doctoral level. It will help justify the time and effort that will be spent on its completion. A carefully thought out and well-designed chapter 2 will also avoid a "So what, who cares?" response from your chair and your committee.

Chapter 3: The Methodology

In your third chapter, the design of the study and how it will respond to the problem so carefully articulated in chapter 1 and supported with a thorough literature review in chapter 2 is described. This chapter clarifies each step of the research plan designed to respond to the topic clearly summarized in the statement of the problem section of chapter 1. This chapter can be fairly brief. It is not uncommon for chapter 3 to be twelve to twenty pages in length.

Introduction

Chapter 3 begins with a brief introduction reviewing the purpose of the study. This helps to once again focus on the topic of the study. This section should describe the purpose by using wording identical to that used to describe the purpose(s) in chapter 1. Exact repetition avoids any possibility of misleading the reader by subtly changing the meaning through the use of similar words.

Description of Methodology Selected

Next, describe the research methodology. How does it relate to the topic? Briefly describe the type of methodology you have elected to use (e.g., experimental, descriptive, historical, ex post facto, and so on) and any variations of the methodology (e.g., a modification of the Delphi technique or a quasi-experimental design).

It is important to remember that the nature of the problem determines the type of research that is best to use in a study. It is not uncommon for the research methodology to be a combination or variety of methodologies. Depending on the nature of the problem, it may be perfectly acceptable for the research methodology to be described as a "mixed methodology."

All too often, a researcher is familiar with a certain type of design and wants to use that design regardless of the topic or problem. This is like putting the cart before the horse. An experimental design is used basically to test causal relationships between two or more variables concerned with "what will be" rather than "what is." This type of design, although neat and tidy, can't be used to obtain facts or to make judgments about existing situations and would not be a suitable design to use in the XYZ Corporation study. A descriptive study would be more appropriate. The nature of the problem always determines the methodology to be used.

Design of the Study

The next item in chapter 3 is the "Design of the Study." In it, the operationalization of the methodological variables is discussed. This section is generally rather brief. For a historical study, this section could discuss how the primary and secondary sources used were identified and/or obtained. In a simple experimental design, the operationalization of variables such as the control and experimental groups as well as the treatment would be discussed.

In the descriptive methodology most likely used in the XYZ Corporation study, a discussion of how the surveys were executed; how, where, and when interviews were conducted; or the nature of any direct observations that may have been made is presented.

Sample and Population

Next comes a discussion of the sample and population or source of data. In the XYZ study, the population is the XYZ Corporation labor and management force. The population for this study would, naturally, be drawn from the company. Ideally, the population would be the entire labor and management force, but if the population is too large or if it is otherwise impossible to obtain results from the entire population, a sample of the population can be used because a properly selected sample can provide meaningful information about the entire population.

In addition to discussing the population or sample used in the study, this section may discuss other appropriate sources of data obtained through various measures, such as counting absences, new enrollments, observing various phenomena, conducting content analyses (the systemic analysis of communications), and objective testing.

Instrumentation

All instruments used in the study are discussed in this section. The purpose of a research instrument is to gather data. The choice of instruments selected to obtain the data is made after the methodology has been determined. Instruments may be verbal (e.g., structured interview forms used by an interviewer), paper and pencil (e.g., a written questionnaire), or more sophisticated electronic tests such as polygraph tests. Regardless of the type of instrument(s) used, it needs to be discussed in this section.

Quite possibly, the literature reviewed in chapter 2 will have identified a variety of instruments appropriate for use in the study. In the proposal, the researcher should have discussed the instruments, determined their reliability (e.g., are they accurate, stable, and will they repeatedly produce the same type of data?), their validity (e.g., to what extent do the instrument or instruments measure what they purport to measure?), their possible applicability to the study, and how they seemed to respond to the study purposes.

For those instruments actually used in the study, there is a need to present this information in the past tense as well as to present the data regarding the reliability and validity of the instruments. This information usually can be obtained from the manuals that accompany the instruments.

Appropriate instruments for the XYZ Corporation study would be those that perform needs assessment and that measure perception. Ideally, you would find instruments that have been used in child-care studies related to industry.

If the instruments that have been discovered are not appropriate for the purposes of the study, it will be necessary to develop instruments specifically for the study. As any research text will point out, this is not an easy process, as it requires a great deal of additional time and effort to research possible test items, construct and revise questionnaires, conduct validation and reliability studies, and conduct pilot testing before the instrument is valid and reliable.

More than 11,000 commercially available educational, personality, aptitude, neuropsychological, achievement, and intelligence tests and instruments of all sorts are reviewed in *Mental Measurements Yearbook* and *Tests in Print* series of the Buros Institute of Mental Measurements. Since its founding in 1938, the institute has been dedicated to monitoring the quality of commercially published tests and providing accurate evaluations of the usefulness and effectiveness of these tests. This material, which is updated frequently, greatly assists learners with the selection of instruments or tests needed to complete their research project and is a superb resource for any researcher. For obvious reasons, these volumes are a gold mine and should be consulted when seeking information about available and appropriate instruments. For the most recent information regarding the Buros Institute publications, check www.unl.edu/buros.

Another wonderful source of test information is the Education Testing Service (ETS). This organization maintains information on more than 20,000 commercial and research instruments. Unlike the Buros Institute, ETS does not evaluate instruments. More information about ETS is available at www.ets.org.

Data Collection and Other Procedures

A discussion of the data-collection procedures and techniques is in the next-to-last section of chapter 3 of the thesis/dissertation. Within this section, the various procedures and techniques used in the study are presented. *Procedures* generally describe the way in which the data were gathered. *Techniques* refer to the ways in which the data were recorded.

As research follows a logical pattern, the research method selected for the study determines how the data will be collected. Data are usually collected in one of three ways: asking questions, observing, or testing. If the study is designed to identify causal relationships between two or more variables, for example, the data-collection procedures would involve gathering quantifiable data from test scores, observations, ratings, or measurements.

In the XYZ Corporation study, which is descriptive in nature, the data-gathering procedures could involve the use of interviews, document analysis, comparisons, correlational studies, and/or evaluations.

Data Analysis

The plan for analyzing the data is the concluding section in the methodology chapter. Following the discussion of the procedures and techniques used to collect the data comes the discussion of the data analysis plan for the study. The purpose of this section is to demonstrate how the data analysis plan responds to the research questions or hypotheses. Few things are more frustrating to the researcher than to realize after data collection has been concluded that the data needed to test a specific hypothesis or research question were not collected or were not conducive to a particular type of analysis or statistical procedure. It is impossible to recollect the data. For this reason, it is essential that in the proposal, the data analysis plan be well thought out and clearly connected to the problem statement, the purposes of the study, the research questions, and/or the hypotheses.

When appropriate, this section also discusses the descriptive and inferential statistical procedures that were used, how they were treated, and how the level of statistical significance used to guide the analysis was determined.

Chapter 4: Presentation and Analysis of the Data

The presentation and analysis of the data is done in the fourth chapter of the thesis/dissertation. In the proposal, this information was briefly mentioned in chapter 3. The contents could not be fully discussed at that time, as the study had not been completed—there was no way of knowing what the data would look like, what trends might possibly emerge, how the research questions would be answered, or if the hypotheses would be accepted or rejected. The length of this chapter in the thesis/dissertation totally depends on the amount and depth of analysis being presented.

The purpose of chapter 4 is to present the findings specifically as related to the research questions or hypotheses. Data are presented in such a way that the reader will be able to draw independent conclusions from the data. If the data are presented correctly and fully, the reader's conclusions should match those developed and presented by the researcher.

Because there are considerable differences of opinion regarding the format of this chapter, it is once again suggested that you become familiar with your graduate school and department policies and procedures, and consult with your advisor and committee prior to developing this chapter.

Findings are usually reported in a narrative format and supplemented with charts, tables, figures, graphs, numbers, and so on. They generally are grouped and presented in sections responsive to the research questions or hypotheses. Charts, figures, and tables are not self-evident and must be presented with text that explains, highlights, or draws attention to salient points relative to the research questions or hypotheses.

Regardless of how they are presented, all relevant data derived from the study should be reported in an objective, nonevaluative way, free from author bias or editorializing. This preserves the integrity of the data presentation and allows the reader to independently interpret the data and draw conclusions. It also helps separate fact from feelings. Although the researcher may be surprised, shocked, disappointed, or have any of a number of emotional reactions to the data, they are reported objectively. If 23 percent of the population indicated something in a certain way, and for some reason this is surprising to the researcher, it is reported factually (i.e., "Twenty-three percent of the population indicated . . ."). Words or comments expressing surprise (i.e., "*Only* 23 percent of the population indicated . . ." or "Isn't it surprising that 23 percent of the population indicated . . . ?") have no place in this section of the chapter. When reporting the findings, the words of Sergeant Joe Friday, from the old *Dragnet* television series—"Just the facts, ma'am. Just the facts!"—are appropriate.

Generally, the factual presentation is kept separate from the inferences, interpretations, or other analytical treatment of the data. In some instances, data presentation and analysis are integrated throughout the chapter. The format of this chapter depends to a large extent on the nature of the data and the topic or problem of the study. If it is important for the reader to have all the data before conclusions can be drawn, then all the data are presented in one section followed by a section presenting the author's analysis or interpretation.

Chapter 5: Summary, Conclusions, and Recommendations

The summary, conclusions, and recommendations relating to the topic of the study are presented in the fifth chapter. The summary is a brief recap of the problem, the major themes on which the literature review was developed, the methodology, and the findings. This serves to refocus the reader on the topic of the study.

If conclusions were not drawn in chapter 4, they are drawn here. The conclusions are one of the more important parts of the study because they provide partial responses to the research questions or provide the basis for accepting or rejecting the hypotheses.

It is essential that the findings and conclusions be tied to the theoretical framework and research questions or hypotheses described in chapter 1. How do the findings and conclusions of the study relate to the theoretical framework? Are they supported by the theory? Do they seem to differ from similar studies using essentially the same theory?

If conclusions were drawn in chapter 4, they need to be summarized and restated in chapter 5. If conclusions were not made in chapter 4, they need to be firmly presented in this chapter. Any additional insights or inspirations derived from the analysis should also be included.

The chapter ends with recommendations. There are usually two types of recommendations: those drawn directly from and supported by the data presented in the study (e.g., suggestions for changing policy, creating new programs, or implementing other findings relative to the XYZ Corporation), and those peripherally related (e.g., suggestions for future research).

Implementation of recommendations directly related to the data may have an immediate impact on the problem or topic of the study. Recommendations relating to future research may complete the research cycle and serve to assist another researcher in responding to a similarly related problem or topic.

References and Appendixes

The thesis or dissertation ends with sections for references and appendixes. Essentially, the references provide the reader with a list of sources used in the study. The sources may have been directly quoted and so indicated in the text, or they may have provided background information that contributed to the development of the topic or methodology. Appendixes include materials, such as earlier versions of questionnaires; cover letters sent to participants in the study; interview guides; results of pilot studies; or graphs, charts, and tables that provide more detailed information than that which is included in the text.

Concluding Thoughts

As discussed earlier, chapter 1 of the proposal remains basically the same in the completed thesis or dissertation with the exception of tense changes from the future to the past.

Chapter 2 may change from the proposal to the final report to include additional literature reflecting unexpected or unanticipated results derived from the data analysis. For example, let's assume that in the XYZ Corporation study, the data revealed a much greater difference in the perception of needs of the child-care program by female managers than the literature review would have suggested. When preparing the final report, it makes good sense to include any additional literature that might help to explain this. A more extensive literature search, using different descriptors, may reveal other studies with similar results. This additional literature is included in the final report, as it provides a more complete basis for analyzing and interpreting the data.

In a well-designed proposal, chapter 3 will be a fairly complete outline for the conduct of the study. Except for the change of tense and other changes reflecting exactly what happened as opposed to what was predicted to happen, chapter 3 in the final report will look very similar to chapter 3 of the proposal.

8

THE DEFENSE

> As an undergraduate, escape was my primary goal; memorize, regurgitate, and graduate was my motto. More schooling and another degree were not in my plans. Five years later I was back. I completed my master's and am now in a PhD program. I have completed the first draft of my dissertation and am actually looking forward to the defense. Soon it will all be over.
>
> I have long since decided that while education isn't exactly wasted on young undergraduates, it is much more fulfilling the second or third time around.
>
> —*Craig*

The thesis or dissertation is now complete. It has been accepted by your chair, the committee, the department, and the graduate school. You have worked hard to produce a quality document that not only adds to the knowledge base but also demonstrates your ability to produce a significant piece of research adhering to an accepted research design. Regardless of whether you have completed the degree online or on-campus, you are now faced with "the defense."

Few things evoke more fear in graduate students than the defense. Horror stories are rampant of students struggling for years to complete the dissertation only to fail the defense: years of work wasted; hours and hours of work all for naught; a monumental waste of time, money, and effort; lives ruined; marriages destroyed; and on and on. It is absolutely amazing how much this has grown out of proportion!

It is rare that one fails the defense. Although it does occasionally happen, it is an infrequent occurrence and one that probably could, and probably should, have been avoided. In this chapter, we'll take a closer look at the purpose of the defense and present some techniques and strategies to make sure you are one of the vast, vast majority who successfully pass the defense.

Understanding the Defense

Historically, the purpose of the defense was to assure that the work being defended was original and that the student was the author and was truly worthy of joining a very elite community of scholars. To accomplish these objectives, very formal examinations were scheduled. Often, to ensure the integrity of the process, visiting scholars who were not connected with the student or the university in any way were invited to participate in the examination process.

The preparation process took a great deal of time and energy. During this time, the haggard countenance of the individual was a dead giveaway that this person was preparing for his or her final defense.

Questions designed to elicit evidence of the student's mastery of all aspects of the content, including the research design; literature related to the study; data analysis; or the ability to compare, contrast, analyze, synthesize, and integrate were considered fair game at many defenses. All committee members asked questions, often with little or no regard to the stress or tension they produced. When one examiner finished, the next began. The examinee was expected to answer every question correctly, thereby demonstrating a full command of both the research process and subject matter mastery.

There were other competing dynamics at work during the examination as well. Frequently, the members vied among themselves to impress one another. It became a matter of personal and professional pride for committee members to demonstrate depth and breadth of knowledge through obtuse questions related to obscure references. Discussions regarding minor points often took on major proportions.

It was no wonder that, in this context, horror stories of students completely falling apart during the exam or failing horribly were commonplace. The reality, however, was that most stories were more fiction than fact. Today, defenses are much more civilized.

This is not to say that failures are a thing of the past. Although it is uncommon, there are still enough examples of individuals failing their final defense to discourage anyone from treating this experience lightly or taking it for granted.

The truth is that if you have made it this far, failure is very unlikely. By this stage, grad students should be pretty well known by the school and their committee. Having worked carefully, skillfully, and tactfully with committee and department personnel, and having responded in an acceptable manner to all concerns raised, one is unlikely to get to the defense without being relatively sure of the anticipated result.

Most committee members want learners to pass and join the ranks of scholars and practitioners who are leaders in the field. Few things give a major advisor, committee chair, or committee member a better feeling than the understanding that student success is due in some small measure to their efforts. Speaking from my own experience, I realize a tremendous sense of pride and satisfaction when one of my advisees successfully completes the dissertation oral.

Preparing for the Defense

It should be noted that most graduate students in traditional on-campus degree programs will experience a face-to-face defense. If you have completed your degree program in an online program, it is common for the defense to be conducted via a conference call.

Many of the techniques and tips presented in Chapter 6 regarding preparation for the oral examination are also useful when preparing for the defense. It may be well to review them before proceeding with this section.

A Meeting with Peers

Remember to try to control as many aspects of the defense process as is possible. To do this, psychologically view the defense as a discussion among peers rather than as a very formal examination. The thesis or dissertation defense is probably the one time you *really* do know more about the topic than your committee does. After all, you conducted the study, analyzed the data, and wrote the final report. You should be the most knowledgeable person available regarding the topic. Be proud of the study and don't be intimidated or let anyone belittle your work.

Know What Is in Your Study

While preparing for the defense, not only do you need to know the sources that have been cited, you also need to know everything about the content and format of the study. If it is in the thesis or dissertation, it is fair game for the defense.

Look carefully at each chapter. What are the various components of the chapters? Why are they included? What is the significance of each subsection? Why were some subsections included and others omitted? Does the literature review provide a complete review of all themes or topics related to the topic? Does it provide a context for your study? What is the theoretical framework that guides the study? Is the rationale for the methodology sound and well developed? Have all relevant data been presented? Are the conclusions data based? How are they related to the theoretical framework? How are they related to the statement of the problem, the purposes of the study, and the research questions or hypotheses? Are there any additional recommendations that could have been included?

Be sure to be able to explain any technical terms in clear, nontechnical language. This is especially important, as it is possible that outside members of the committee may not understand the technical language and may ask questions in that regard. Don't use jargon and clichés when explaining terms. Also, remember that form follows content and that there are no hard-and-fast rules about how many chapters are needed or about what belongs in each chapter. At this point, you need to be able to explain the study in terms of its particular content and format. As has been stated several times before, however, you need to check the policies and procedures of your school to be sure of what is being asked of you regarding the form, style, and content of your thesis or dissertation.

Play "devil's advocate" with yourself and identify as many weaknesses as possible. Be hard on yourself. Try to develop points counter to those stressed in your study. Know the arguments and references of those who may support a different theoretical framework or perspective.

Involve Others

One of the best ways to prepare for the defense is to ask friends, family, fellow learners, and/or coworkers to read your study and raise any questions or concerns they may have about anything you have written. Often, these people will provide fresh insight or raise concerns that can only be brought up by someone who knows little or nothing about the topic.

In Chapter 5, the roles and responsibilities of committee members were presented. As mentioned, it is common for one of the members (usually the dean's representative) to be appointed or selected from outside your field. When preparing for the defense, an advantage of involving a friend, family member, or colleague with little knowledge about your topic is that this person may raise questions similar to those the dean's representative may raise. If this happens, don't jump down his or her throat or otherwise take advantage of a close relationship. Keep your cool and be thankful that the issue was raised now rather than by a committee member.

The Mock Defense

Another good way to prepare is to have a "mock defense" that is similar to the format that will be used in your defense. A mock defense is a simulation activity wherein a panel of knowledgeable individuals (usually fellow grad students) is assembled and simulates a defense by acting as your committee. Many times, the questions posed by fellow students are more difficult and demanding than those asked by the committee. The obvious advantage of a mock defense is that there is little to be lost and much to be gained through this experience.

Know Your Committee

Don't forget to consult with your chair about the defense. Get his or her thoughts about how defenses are conducted. What is the accepted protocol? What is the chair's role in this process? In some colleges, the chair consults extensively with the other committee members and the dean or graduate college representative to determine the questions or concerns that may be raised and attempts to screen them to ensure that they are directly related to the work being presented. Others seemingly care little about the questions that may be raised and facilitate the defense so that each committee member has ample time to raise each and every concern, even if they have little relationship to your thesis or dissertation. It is always best to consult with your chair for any advice that can be given about the possible questions or concerns that may be raised, the communication style, and the research interests of the committee members, as well as any information that can be shared about the "outsiders" (the dean's representative or the graduate college representative) who may be present.

It also makes sense to find out as much as possible about the outside member of your committee. Check his or her reputation with other graduate students, faculty, and staff. Go to the library or conduct an online search and review the publications of this person. When appropriate, weave this knowledge into your responses. Not only does this give the committee member a possible ego boost, it also helps you to remain in control, as it demonstrates to the committee that you take the process seriously.

The worst-case scenario would be that your chair will share nothing with you. In most cases, careful and tactful probing will produce valuable information about the concerns of the committee members and the process and the content of the defense.

Don't overlook this opportunity to consult directly with the other committee members as another means of preparing for the defense. Use the same type of careful and tactful probing to solicit their advice. Again, you can lose nothing and usually will gain a great deal.

Consult with Recent Graduates

Check with others who have recently been through a defense in your department. This is a very meaningful discussion topic to introduce to the "Thursday evening grad student get-together" or online discussion group mentioned in Chapter 6. What were their experiences? Which professors asked the most difficult questions?

Who asked the easy ones? How helpful or how much of a problem was Professor X, who also happens to be on your committee?

Regardless of who is asked and how reliable this person is, remember that this person is not you and that he or she has not produced your study. All anyone can do is to provide advice based on personal experience. It is your job to process it to help in your preparation. Don't take advice as gospel and fail to fully prepare simply because a fellow graduate student said that Professor X didn't ask "that type of question." Maybe that was so in his or her defense, but it doesn't mean that it will be so for you. It is much better to overprepare and be disappointed that certain questions were not asked than to underprepare and wish that you had done a better job of preparation.

Attend Other Defenses

The length of a defense may vary anywhere from forty-five minutes to a few hours. There is no set way in which it is conducted. In some graduate colleges, the process is described quite clearly in policy guidelines, but in others, the department or a committee develops the process.

In some enlightened graduate colleges, the defense is open to all and is publicized as a learning opportunity for the community of scholars. In others, it is an activity closed to all but you and your committee.

If they are available, take the opportunity to attend as many defenses as possible. Try to attend those where your chair and other committee members may be observed in action. How do they seem to react to the student? Are they overly concerned with impressing others with their knowledge? Are they supportive? What types of questions do they ask? Are they more concerned with process than content? Do they seem to have a consistent pattern of raising questions or concerns?

As a courtesy, it makes good sense to check with the person whose defense it is to see if your presence would be a problem. When the defense is open to all, it creates more stress for most students, regardless of how well they have prepared. Anything to help a colleague at this time is always appreciated.

In some cases, your presence might not be welcomed. The only way to know for certain is to ask the person involved.

What to Do at the Defense

Prepare carefully for the defense. Don't assume anything. At my university, it is perfectly appropriate (and, indeed, encouraged) for learners to have their thesis or dissertation with them at the oral. We recognize that the purpose of the oral is to demonstrate mastery of what you have written and how you developed the study. We don't expect that learners will memorize everything in the study. We encourage learners to make marginal notes and to have resources with them if they so desire. It is amazing to me how many students believe that none of this is allowed. Where does this idea come from? It certainly isn't in the learner handbook or other policy documents. I imagine that they *assume* this just isn't allowed. Wrong!

Play the Name Game

Just like the oral exam, know every source or reference in your study. This is also called "playing the name game." Be absolutely sure you know who said what and why it was said. If a particular name or reference has been included in your study, it is your responsibility to know what the author is saying and how it relates to your work.

Often, graduate students blithely include in their study all the sources or references that happen to be cited in a related article or research report. If the author thought it was important, it probably was. What is not known for certain is the author's motivation. All that is known is that the author of the article or report included the additional sources.

Including sources identified in this manner can lead to trouble in the defense, particularly if a committee member happens to be familiar with these sources. It is embarrassing to be totally unfamiliar with an author or reference cited in your study. Avoid this by spending the extra needed time to become familiar with all sources. Check to see if URLs cited in your study are current. Web sources have a habit of disappearing with little or no notice. Checking them out and being able to tell your committee that they are not currently available is yet another indication of your thoroughness. Although this will surely require additional time, it is worth it.

How to Respond to Questions

RESPONDING TO QUESTIONS

1. Answer like a witness on the stand.
2. Avoid monosyllabic answers.
3. "I don't know but . . ."
4. Refer to your study.

First, remember the tips you used when you took the oral part of your comprehensive exam (discussed in Chapter 6).

Let's assume that everything suggested in this chapter to prepare for the defense has been done. The introductions are over and the first question has been asked. What do you do? Again, controlling the process as much as possible is the key to success.

Answer Like a Witness on the Stand. One way to maintain control is to think of yourself as a witness on the stand at a trial. Lawyers prepare witnesses by telling them to answer the question honestly but to volunteer nothing. This rationale is to force the other side to be very clear about what is being asked. At the defense, your role is not to sidestep the issue but to provide only what is being asked for and not to give more information than is required.

Although the defense should not be viewed as an adversarial relationship between you and your committee, answering the question in as few words as possible, but as fully as possible, makes good sense. This forces the committee members to more clearly articulate points they want elaborated.

By volunteering more than is called for, you may provide a committee member with additional information to develop another question. Recognize that the committee members are quite capable of developing their own questions and that you are possibly hurting yourself by raising concerns they may not have considered.

Avoid Monosyllabic Responses. Rather than responding with monosyllabic statements, answer the question as fully as possible and with as much conviction as possible. Exhibit confidence and self-assurance.

Even with the most extensive preparation, it is likely that you will be asked about something with which you are not familiar. Committees expect this and are generally more receptive to an honest response rather than one in which you try to bluff your way through it.

I Don't Know But . . . A better way to respond to a question to which the answer is unknown might be something like this: "I'm not certain of the answer to that question but here is my thinking on it" or "I'm not sure but here's how I would go about getting the information. I would go to such and such a book and look it up or I might do a search of the literature using descriptors such as. . . ."

Used judiciously, the "I don't know but" approach actually can be positive because it can demonstrate that you are in control, not intimidated, and would proceed to develop a response in an acceptable, scholarly manner .

Refer to Your Study. Another useful strategy is to remember that questions may be asked that are clearly answered in the thesis or dissertation. A frequent reaction is to think the questioner has not read the study; otherwise, that question would not have been asked. Maybe this is so, but don't second-guess the reason for the question. Respond to it. Carefully handled, this situation can provide another opportunity to demonstrate that you are "in charge."

For example, assume that a question has been asked that is directly answered by a chart that appears in chapter 4 of the study. Being very familiar with your work, you know it is in that chapter. As part of your response, skillfully, carefully, and tactfully direct the attention of the committee to the right section or page of the study where the answer appears; then proceed to answer the question. Handled well, this demonstrates obvious familiarity with your work and your concern for not embarrassing the committee member in front of colleagues by pointing out that he or she has perhaps not fully read the work or may have missed the obvious answer to the question.

The Decision

Sooner or later, the defense will be over. At the end of the defense, it is not uncommon for the chair to ask that you excuse yourself from the proceedings to give the committee an opportunity to discuss the defense and make a decision. When defenses are open learning events, the committee may seclude itself or conduct this part of the defense in private. This is usually the time when a formal vote is taken and a decision is made.

If all goes well, the committee reconvenes, offers its congratulations, and begins the process of welcoming you to the community of scholars. If the results are not positive, you will be told of the results and the available options.

Occasionally, as a result of substantive and editorial concerns that may have been raised at the defense, it is not uncommon for the committee to delay or postpone the decision and to request that additional changes be made in the thesis or dissertation. When these have been made and accepted by the committee, some universities reconvene the committee to review the changes. In others, the chair reviews the revised work and makes the decision regarding the processing of the final papers.

When the university has been assured that all relevant policies and procedures have been completed, you are done and are ready to graduate. Congratulations!

9

NOW WHAT?

> I don't think anything prepared me for the impact graduate school would have on various aspects of my life—most particularly regarding my relationship with my spouse.
>
> Only after a rather serious discussion with my committee chair and a group of fellow students did I even become aware of how my relationship with my husband was being shortchanged. I realized that sharing allowed him to feel included in the process. That helped the two of us get through some pretty rough spots.
>
> —*Mary Ann*

Completion of a graduate degree puts you in a rather elite group of college graduates. You have worked hard and should feel proud of yourself. All the time and effort have paid off. Objectives have been set and accomplished. Although the hard part is over, a few things still need to be considered.

Binding Your Thesis or Dissertation

Even if it is not required by your university, consider having several copies of your thesis or dissertation bound with a hard cover and embossed with the title and your name on the spine and on the front cover. With the preponderance of desktop publishing programs, it is quite easy to revise the format of your study so it looks as though it were a printed book. Binding provides a way of permanently preserving your study. A gift of a bound copy is also a meaningful way to thank your committee chair and members for their help. It is a particularly significant way to show your appreciation to "significant others," such as parents, spouse, or others without whose help the degree might not have been completed.

Library binding companies provide this service and are usually found in the local phone directory or through a Web search using "library binding" as the search topic. Many commercial duplicating services also provide binding services. Public libraries are always having books rebound and can supply the names and addresses of local companies that may provide this service. The college or university library or bookstore may also be able to provide leads for this service.

Copyrighting Your Work

Many graduate programs require that all studies be copyrighted. This is for your protection in the unlikely event that someone may claim your study or parts therein as his or her own. Information regarding copyrighting your material can be obtained from the following agency:

Copyright Office
Library of Congress
101 Independence Avenue, S.E.
Washington, DC 20559-6000
(202) 707-3000
www.copyright.gov

A copyright is a form of intellectual property law provided by the laws of the United States (title 17, U.S. Code) to authors of "original works of authorship," including both published and unpublished works, including your thesis or dissertation. It grants owners of a copyright the sole and exclusive right to do or to allow others to do such things as reproduce all or part of the work, distribute copies, prepare new versions based on the original work, and to perform and display the work publicly. Even if you are not required to copyright your work, do it anyway. It is a relatively inexpensive process and will provide protection for your work.

In some instances, the outcome of a thesis or dissertation is a new product, idea, or discovery that may be worth money. By copyrighting your work, it will be protected to the fullest extent of the law.

Questions and Answers on Copyright for the Campus Community is a guide developed to help campuses conform to the requirements of U.S. copyright law. The guide is sponsored and copyrighted by the National Association of College Stores (NACS), the Association of American Publishers, and the Software Publishers Association and has been endorsed by the Association of American University Presses and the Copyright Clearance Center. The goal of the seventh edition of the guide, published in 2006, is to provide information in a clear and concise manner relative to the complexities of copyright law. More information can be obtained through the NACS Store (www.nacs.org/nacs_store) click on "Textbooks and Course Materials" in the "Browse by Category" pull-down menu; then scroll down and click on "Questions and Answers on Copyright for the Campus Community" in the "Matching Items" pull-down menu. You can also write to the association at:

National Association of College Stores, Inc.
500 E. Loraine Street
Oberlin, OH 44074-1295

Publishing Your Work

Everyone who has ever completed a thesis or dissertation wants to have it commercially published. Very few ever do. Only three of my doctoral advisees and one of my master's advisees have been successful in having their work published as a book by a reputable publisher. In all cases, they spent more than a year following graduation working to revise their work into formats that were acceptable to their publishers. If you really want to have your work published in a book format but cannot secure a contract from a recognized and reputable publisher, there are several companies that will work with you to self-publish your study as a book. These sources can be found through a Web search using "self-publishing" as the descriptor.

It is much more common for studies to be reworked into an article that is published by a professional or scholarly journal. In this regard, several of my advisees, at both the master's and the doctoral levels, have had articles published based on their graduate work.

It is important to the field for graduate students who have produced a particularly good thesis or dissertation to disseminate the results of their work. The study abstract is a good starting point for the development of an article. However, before completely developing the article, review the professional journals to determine acceptable formats. Most journals or scholarly publications provide guidelines for authors on request.

Your committee chair and members are another source of assistance in developing the article and getting it published. However, when working with one or more of your committee on the development of a book or article based on your study, or with any coauthor, consider the following procedural and ethical questions:

1. Who is the primary author, you or your advisor?
2. How do you determine if your advisor should receive recognition as a coauthor?
3. How will you split royalties?

The answers to these questions are based on such considerations as the amount of work expended on idea development, research, identification and review of the literature, and other logistical concerns. If your major advisor has made the primary contribution to the development of the work, then he or she legitimately should be primary author. However, if you have done the majority of the work, you should be listed as primary author. If publishing is an intended outcome of your work, answers to these questions should be determined as early as possible.

The three authors of *Teaching and Learning Basic Skills: A Guide for Adult Basic Education and Developmental Education Programs* (Rossman, Fisk, and Roehl, 1984) are two former doctoral advisees and myself. In 1980 I received a grant to produce a manual for teachers of adults in Arizona. The grant provided funds for two research assistants. I interviewed several candidates and hired two doctoral candidates in my department. Under my direction, we researched the needs of teachers of adults in Arizona; reviewed existing literature, including material from other states; and developed, field-tested, and evaluated drafts of material responsive to these needs. The ultimate product was a field-tested manual for teachers of adults in Arizona.

From the beginning, it was my desire to publish the results of our work in the form of appropriate articles or a book. I discussed this with each of the candidates interviewed for the research assistantships and also received permission from the funding source to publish the manual as a book, giving credit as appropriate. One of the first things we did when the team was finalized was discuss how to operationalize this notion. Among other things, we decided that as I had conceived and developed the idea, directed the project, written much of the material, and reviewed everything that was produced, I should be primary author. We also determined a procedure for listing who would be the second and third authors and how royalties would be split.

Once the manual was produced, our obligation to the funding source was complete. As we planned, I sent letters to various publishers. Eventually, Teachers College Press of Columbia University published a greatly modified version of the manual. When the book was published, there were no hurt feelings or bruised egos because the three of us had raised questions and developed solutions right from the start of the project. This created an atmosphere of mutual trust and respect. The research assistants found a way to help finance their graduate degrees and also experienced their first publication. I was able to record another professionally significant entry on my résumé.

No discussion of publishing would be complete without mentioning the Educational Resources Information Center (ERIC). This ERIC data base contains more than 1.3 million bibliographic records of education-related materials and is actively seeking submissions of high-quality materials. Owners of copyright materials, such as a thesis or dissertation, are encouraged to submit this material to ERIC. More information is available at www.eric.ed.gov.

In Chapter 7 I mentioned ProQuest as a source for finding completed theses and dissertations. Did you ever wonder how those theses and dissertations got there? Many colleges and universities routinely arrange for the final draft of your work to be sent to ProQuest so that it is available to others who may be interested in your study. ProQuest microfilms your dissertation, includes it in its Web-based digital file, and publishes it upon request, thus assuring that academic researchers around the world will have access to your work. There is a cost for this service that is frequently included as part of your graduation fee. If your college or university does not have such an arrangement, you can pay the fee and submit your approved draft, as long as it has been obtained from an accredited program. More information about this is available at disspub@proquest.com.

Making Up Lost "Quality Time"

Now that you have earned a master's or doctoral degree, a major question is this: "What do I do with all the time I used to spend working on my degree?" One of the first things to do is to become "reacquainted" with your family. In most families, many sacrifices have been made for you to complete your graduate degree. Spouses have spent many hours without your company when you have been in class, preparing for an exam, writing your thesis, or researching your dissertation. Probably there were any number of times your spouse or mate surely wanted to go to a movie, go out with friends, go out to dinner, or do anything other than stay home and watch TV and keep quiet.

Although it is true that you alone completed your graduate degree, it probably could not have been done without help, particularly from those you live with. Ideally, you have kept these very important people as involved as possible. As mentioned in Chapter 1, many changes and sacrifices were needed for you to complete this degree. Now that you are done, some show of appreciation is in order. Whether appreciation is demonstrated in the form of something tangible, such as an inscribed bound copy of your thesis or dissertation or other gift of some sort, or in the expression of deeply felt feelings, it is strongly encouraged that you take action to show just how much the efforts of all concerned are appreciated.

Realize, too, the sacrifices of your children. They may well have wanted to spend part of each weekend with you but had to give that up for you to have the needed study time. How many evenings did they do without their mommy or daddy because you were in class or at the library? Maybe they had to be out of the house so you could have quiet when you were working on your computer. Don't forget, it is their home, too.

A classic case in point is that of the four-year-old who on being told that mommy had finished her degree said, "Does that mean I don't have to go to the zoo every weekend anymore and now you can be a real mommy?" How much was said in that sentence?

Commencement

A wonderful way to bring the family together and to formally celebrate completion of the graduate school experience is to attend commencement and to have a graduation party. This is a formal and highly appropriate way to bring closure to life as a graduate student.

In most college and university commencement ceremonies, special attention is given to the recipients of graduate degrees. Many graduate colleges stage an impressive ceremony of "hooding" master's and doctoral degree holders. Each individual name is called out, the proud recipients walk across the stage in full academic regalia, accept the congratulations of the president and chancel party, receive the diploma, and accept the accolades of professors, family, friends, and colleagues.

Following the ceremony, families take pictures and bask in the glory of the graduates. It is a time for joy, and it shouldn't be missed. Commencement provides an opportunity for those special people to share in your happiness. Give yourself and them this opportunity. Go to commencement.

Developing an Unofficial Annotated Transcript

The transcript is the official record kept by the institution awarding the degree of what you did to earn your degree. At most colleges and universities, the transcript contains much, if not all, of the following information: dates of your enrollment, the name of the school and/or program offering the degree (i.e., Capella University, School of Education; Arizona State University, College of Business); name of the degree (i.e., MA in Education, MBA, PhD in Psychology); degree specialization or major (i.e., adult education, English literature, clinical psychology); courses that transferred from other universities; prefix, number, and titles of the courses taken from the institution granting the graduate degree; grades earned; dates of the comprehensive exam, oral exam, and dissertation defense; and title of the thesis or dissertation. Although this may sound like a lot of information, it really doesn't describe what you have learned. It only describes what you did to learn it.

One way to provide more information about what you have learned is to create an *unofficial annotated transcript.* This supplements the official transcript and contains more information than that which is included in the traditional transcript. I have found that students who use an unofficial annotated transcript in conjunction with the portfolio résumé (described in the following sections) tend to have more job interviews than those who do not. One reason for this is that these documents demonstrate that the student is well organized, concerned with detail, and wants to present as much information as possible to the interview committee.

The following is an example of an unofficial annotated transcript for a fictitious learner at Capella University.

Unofficial Annotated Transcript

John Q. Learner

Name

January 2005–May 2008

Dates of Attendance at Capella University

PhD

Degree

Community College

Emphasis Area

Term	Course Description	Instructor	Grade
Winter '05	HD501–Survey of Research in Human Development *Course Description.* This course reviews the major theories of human development and behavior across the entire life cycle. The developing person is the focus of inquiry and connects such areas of study as psychology, anthropology, and biology. Some of the research will approach human development from the point of view of personality theory, developmental tasks, or moral development. *Course Individualization.* I emphasized adult development applied to a community college setting.	Dr. Mark Rossman Instructor Signature Date	S

Unofficial Annotated Transcript (continued)

Term	Course Description	Instructor	Grade
Winter '05	OD501–Survey of Research in Organizational and Group Dynamics *Course Description.* This course is a survey of the theories and research in organizational and group dynamics. It explores the ways in which humans organize themselves into groups and the basic principles that guide the behavior of these organizations. The term organization refers to the nature of human groups. In this sense, organizations include families, gangs, businesses, teams, and other formal and informal groups. This course is designed to create an understanding of the interactive forces of change that influence organizational and social groups. *Course Individualization.* I emphasized work teams in a community college.	Dr. Robert Bacon ________________ Instructor Signature ________________ Date	S

Unofficial Annotated Transcript (continued)

Term	Course Description	Instructor	Grade
Spring '05	ED815–The Future of Educational Institutions *Course Description.* This course concerns research and theories relating to societal and cultural evolution. The dynamics of cultural development are studied within the broader context of societal issues. The study of societal issues emphasizes an understanding of cultural dynamics and change. *Course Individualization.* I emphasized the dynamics of change as applied to my department.	Dr. Bernard Sarone ____________________ Instructor Signature ____________________ Date	S
Spring '05	ED815–The Future of Educational Institutions *Course Description.* Based on an examination of the formative ideas that have shaped educational institutions, this course explores both the theory and practice of changing educational institutions to meet future needs. An understanding of the philosophy of American Education, as well a knowledge of institutional change, will be necessary. *Course Individualization.* I emphasized the changing role of the community college.	Dr. Bernard Sarone ____________________ Instructor Signature ____________________ Date	S

Unofficial Annotated Transcript (continued)

Term	Course Description	Instructor	Grade
Summer '05	ED814–Evaluating the Effectiveness of the Educational Process *Course Description.* This course explores a variety of evaluation techniques to examine the individual educational programs or entire educational systems. It also provides theoretical frameworks on which evaluations are based.	Dr. Keith Johnson ________________ Instructor Signature ________________ Date	S
Winter '06	RM900–Comprehensive *Course Description.* This eight-credit learning experience is designed to demonstrate mastery of the program of study. The written comprehensive is evaluated by the mentor and two faculty members in the field of study. The comprehensive is also evaluated in an oral comprehensive conference. *Course Individualization.* I emphasized the need for the community college to become more effectively involved with the community it serves. I also stressed the need for new administrative and leadership patterns.	Dr. Mark Rossman ________________ Instructor Signature ________________ Date	S

Unofficial Annotated Transcript (continued)

The **Residency Requirement** at Capella university consists of three face-to-face residency colloquia offered several times each year at conference hotels throughout the country. Each colloquia consists of a variety of concurrent academic sessions, specialization meetings, and opportunities to interact with fellow learners and faculty. I attended one of these sessions each year I was enrolled in the program.

Dissertation Title: Skills and Knowledge Needed for Community College Administrators: A Delphi Study.

Dissertation Oral Conference was conducted on May 17, 2006.

Dissertation Committee Members:

Dr. Mark H. Rossman, Chair

Dr. Keith Johnson, Faculty Evaluator

Dr. Duane Arnold, Independent Reviewer

Dr. C. C. President, Visiting Scholar

MS. Ima Student, Learner Peer

____

Signature

____

Date

In this unofficial annotated transcript, the learner has provided much more information about what was learned than what would appear on the traditional transcript. The course descriptions were verbatim from the college catalog. Each course was individualized to reflect the major or specialization area. The name of the instructor was listed. The signature of the instructor, if available, indicates that the instructor has approved this description, particularly regarding the way in which the course was individualized. Other unique aspects of the program at Capella University (the comps, the residency, and the committee structure) are also described as further elaboration of what has been learned.

If various parts of the unofficial annotated transcript are not appropriate for you, feel free to omit them and add other sections as needed.

As long as it is not specifically prohibited, the learner could include the unofficial annotated transcript as a supplement to material required for a new job or promotion.

It should be stressed that this is designed to supplement the official transcript, not to replace or supplant it.

The Portfolio Résumé

In many of the commercially available résumé guides, the majority of advice given seems to indicate that the human resources person who will review your résumé is very busy and will only read short (often one-page) résumés. I think this does not do justice to you and the work you have completed to achieve your current status or position. I remember speaking about this to a friend of mine who was a visual artist. He told me that many artists develop a portfolio of their work to show to prospective employers or clients. Eureka! An idea was born.

Over the years, in addition to developing the traditional résumé that includes all the usual data, I have suggested that my advisees develop an expanded or *portfolio résumé* that more fully describes their accomplishments. There is no set pattern of what goes into the portfolio résumé. It needs to reflect you and how you want to present yourself.

Once it is finished, it should be updated any time there is a need to do so. By keeping it up-to-date, you will always be ready to respond when an opportunity presents itself. Many graduates post the portfolio résumé as part of their personal Web page.

A format that has been successful for many is the following.

Portfolio Résumé

1. Personal
   A. A brief résumé listing past positions and responsibilities
   B. Employment Objectives
   C. Student copies of transcripts
      a. undergraduate
      b. master's
      c. doctorate
      d. continuing education
2. Supplemental Information Relative to the Graduate Program
3. Letters of Thanks and Commendations
4. Reports and Publications
5. Miscellaneous Related Professional Material

Personal

Within this section would be things such as the following:

A. A brief résumé listing past positions and responsibilities
B. Employment Objectives
C. Student or unofficial copies of transcripts
   a. undergraduate
   b. master's
   c. doctorate
   d. continuing education

This material is similar to that which is usually called for by respective employers. It is the material that follows this section that takes on a different feeling.

Supplemental Information Relative to the Graduate Program

In this section, information about conferences, workshops, extracurricular lectures, and activities that added to your program but do not show up on the traditional transcript are included. For example, let's say you initiated and monitored a learner discussion group designed to provide support to fellow grad students. This shows a leadership quality that seldom presented in the traditional résumé. Maybe you supervised a student teacher or intern. This could be included in this section along with a brief description of what you did and what you learned as related to your overall degree objectives.

Selected Letters of Thanks and Commendation

Many of us have received thank-you notes from clients for a service that has been performed in the course of our job. It is not unusual for a conference coordinator or team leader to send commendation letters or certificates of appreciation to those who have made the event or conference a success. What happens to these notes and commendations? Many are kept in a shoe box or in the upper left-hand drawer of the desk until they are thrown away. Take time to collect and list this material in chronological order and include the list in this section. Don't limit the list to job-related events. Volunteer work that is not job-related demonstrates the type of person you are. Go back as far as you can. The not-so-hidden objective of this bit of bravado is to provide evidence about you as a individual in your community as well your work habits and ethics. Sure, one or two isolated notes ten years apart might not show much about you, but if you can put together a list of ten, fifteen, or more, a side of your personality emerges that is not seen in most traditional résumés.

Reports and Publications

Many of my graduates seek jobs in academia. An important requisite for this type of position often relates to publications and professional presentations. Think about the class papers you have developed. Many of them demonstrate an academic competence or pattern that is often overlooked. You have worked hard on those papers. If they reflect the type of work you are capable of doing and will add substance to your portfolio résumé, add them to this section.

How about those human resource reports or the fiscal analyses you have completed over the years? Do they reflect your style? Put them in this section.

A suggested format for this section for one seeking an academic position might be as follows:

A. Books
B. Reports
C. Media Publications
   a. Films
   b. Cassettes
   c. Video
D. Power Point Presentations
E. Chapter and Articles

Miscellaneous Related Professional Material

This is the proverbial "kitchen sink." Anything that provides additional evidence about interests, skills, and abilities that has not been included elsewhere in the portfolio résumé goes into this section. Newspaper articles, interviews, nominations of various sorts, appointments of volunteer boards, honors, and so on are all fair game for this area.

Remember that there are no required sections in the portfolio résumé. Its main purpose is to provide additional insights and information to a prospective employer or client regarding you, your skills, abilities and personality. If the suggested sections don't reflect you, feel free to discard them and add others.

Table of Contents and Cover Letter

Once you have completed your portfolio résumé, develop a single-spaced Table of Contents. At the top of the page, provide your contact information (name, address, phone numbers, and e-mail address). Then write a cover letter on your personal letterhead using the following as a guide.

Portfolio Résumé Cover Letter

(written on your personal letterhead)

Date

Dr. Mr. Ms. ______________________________, Chair of Selection Committee

Name of the Institution

Street Address

City, State and ZIP

Dear ______________________________,

Enclosed is the Table of Contents to my portfolio résumé. I am enclosing this as part of my application for the position of (write in the job or position).

Since (fill in the year of the earliest entry), I have kept a portfolio relevant to my professional growth and development. These items provide a more complete understanding of me, my skills, interests, and abilities as related to (write in the job or position).

I believe my portfolio résumé describes me much more fully than the traditional résumé as it presents a fuller description of my background and experience. I would be pleased to send copies of any item in my portfolio résumé to you and/or any member of the selection committee. You may view it on my home page at (provide the address of your home page). Please feel free to contact me at the address above.

Yours very truly,

Name ______________________________

Title ______________________________

When you apply for a position, pay careful attention to the posted requirements of the position and be sure to provide everything that is called for in your cover letter. Unless it is explicitly prohibited, include the contents of the portfolio résumé cover letter as well. Many of my graduates have used this approach and have gotten proportionally more interviews than those who have limited themselves to using the traditional résumé format. Once you have the interview, it is up to you to present yourself as well as possible.

The portfolio résumé provides prospective employers with a much greater sense of who you are. It demonstrates a strong organizational ability if nothing else. Some graduates have told me that they felt they were denied an interview because they used this approach. My response is that if the employer turned you down because of this creative means of providing information, you probably wouldn't be happy there even if you were hired.

Using the Title *Doctor*

Since royalty was eliminated in the United States, the title *Doctor* has been seen by many to be the closest thing this country has to royalty. Power and prestige are often associated with a person holding this title. It is amazing how many receptionists will put through a call from *Dr.* Jones with no screening but will interrogate *Mr.* Jones before putting the call through.

Society frequently views the holder of a doctorate with awe and with a certain amount of deference and respect. After all, only slightly more than one percent of the population over eighteen years of age hold a doctorate. Some holders of the doctorate feel the title gives them credibility and will use it professionally but not socially. Others will use it both professionally and socially. Interestingly, the term *physician* is protected by law in many countries and entitles the holder of an earned medical degree to use "Doctor" or "Dr." as a prefix to his or her name. In recent years, with the proliferation of earned doctoral degrees, holders of most earned doctoral degrees can also use the term with relative impunity.

Many holders of a doctoral degree insist on being referred to as *doctor* by everyone. Although this may be considered by some to be presumptuous, it is not wrong because there is no correct response regarding when to use the title and when not to. Each individual needs to consider his or her situation and his or her own reactions to the use of the title.

ABD—All But Dissertation

When students complete a doctoral program of study as well as the comps, they are admitted to candidacy and are frequently referred to as being "ABD" (*A*ll *B*ut *D*issertation). This designation is so prevalent that many learners list themselves as "ABD" on their résumés after they have completed comps but before having completed the doctorate.

For a variety of reasons, as many as 50 percent of the students who complete comps do not complete the doctorate. Thus, it is not uncommon for an individual to list ABD as his or her highest educational attainment. However, ABD is not a degree, and the feeling of many in academia is that listing ABD on a résumé or curriculum vita is tacky and should be avoided.

Avoiding Emotional Letdowns

Don't be surprised if an emotional letdown accompanies the completion of the degree. This is very common. Ideally, with the degree has come additional knowledge and wisdom. However, you are still basically the same person you were when you started.

An emotional letdown is easy to understand, particularly for those who have completed a doctorate. The title of the old song sung by Peggy Lee, "Is That All There Is?" is particularly poignant at this time. You have spent much of your life going to school. First, you completed primary school and high school. Then, you went to college and completed your bachelor's degree. Graduate school was probably always in the back of your mind. When everything was in place, you were accepted into graduate school and began work on the degree. A lot of time, money, and energy were devoted to this. Many sacrifices were made by you and others. The constant stress of completing and controlling the process has been a part of your life for a considerable period of time. Now this is gone. Although it is good to be relieved of this pressure, its release can create a letdown.

Although many expect sirens to wail and fireworks to emblazon the sky when they complete the degree, this won't happen. Life returns to normal. You have really only just begun and now need to put the new knowledge to work.

One way to avoid the letdown is to plan to use the time formerly devoted to graduate work for other scholarly activity, such as writing the book or article discussed earlier in this chapter (see "Publishing Your Work"). How about taking some of that time and using it to implement the plans or recommendations that were suggested in your study? After all, who knows more about the rationale behind the recommendations? Or use this time to become more involved with a hobby or to read all those mystery books that were put on the shelf until after graduation. Take the family on a vacation. Visit friends you haven't seen for a while. Bring back the weekly dinners with the in-laws. Have a good time.

Put Your Degree to Work

There are many real and perceived changes concurrent with the completion of a graduate degree. Using myself as an example, within one year after having earned both my master's and my doctorate, I had secured new professional positions and was earning significantly more money.

Eric, Gene, and Patrice are three former advisees who negotiated well and benefited greatly from the completion of their degrees. They used their degrees wisely.

As part of a grant we were working on, Eric received an assistantship to develop a series of staff development training modules. He did his job well and produced all that was asked of him. More important, he asked many questions and learned a great deal about the process of researching and writing grants.

After graduation, he secured a university position and proceeded to write grants to finance his own research interests. He became so good that others began to ask for his help in writing grants. Within a few years, Eric wrote and published a book about grant writing. He developed and offered a series of grant-writing workshops around the country and is in great demand as a consultant. He is now a tenured, full professor and well respected in his field.

Gene was a middle-aged businessperson with an MBA and a successful small business when he entered graduate school to work on his PhD. He had been quite interested in the personal well-being of his employees and had spent a great deal of time talking with them. Gene realized that what he really liked best was being able to help people with their problems.

After completing necessary prerequisite courses, he was admitted to a doctoral program in psychology. Through the required core courses, he gained a strong theoretical foundation in psychology. Gene realized he needed more than the usual field experiences to gain additional counseling experience. Being used to negotiating, he arranged not one but three internships in local area mental health facilities. He clearly demonstrated an ability to combine compassion with practicality. After graduation, he was hired by the mental health agency in which he had completed his last internship and successfully made the transition from businessperson to counselor.

Patrice had a bachelor's degree and was working as an administrative assistant in a small Midwestern hospital. It did not take her long to realize that she needed a master's if she was going to experience any career advancement.

She entered a master's degree program with a concentration in human resources. A practicum was required as part of her degree program. Patrice negotiated this experience so she could develop a sorely needed personnel policy manual for her hospital. Once this was developed, with the approval of her chairperson, she also developed, field-tested, and evaluated the manual. The entire process formed the basis of her thesis—a case study describing the development, field-testing, and evaluation of a personnel manual for a small Midwestern hospital.

Shortly after Patrice graduated, the hospital human resource coordinator retired. Because of her graduate work, Patrice was the logical person to be offered the position. She quickly accepted it and is now making a major contribution in her chosen profession.

Eric, Gene, and Patrice are three of many thousands of success stories from individuals like you who have made the decision to complete a graduate degree.

Their lives have changed; their futures are more secure. Like countless others, they were fearful of the unknown when they began, but they used their motivation, desire, and ability to complete their degrees. They did it! They negotiated. They persevered. So can you. Good luck!

REFERENCES AND SUGGESTED READINGS

References

Allen, I. E., and J. Seaman. 2008. *Growing by Degrees: Online Education in the United States, 2005.* Needham, MA: Sloan Consortium.

Basmet, P., L. Lewis, and P. Tice. 2008. *Distance Education at Degree-Granting, Postsecondary Institutions, 2006–07, First Look* (NCES 2009-044). Washington, DC: National Center for Educational Statistics.

Berkner, L., C. C. Wei, S. He, S. Lew, M. Cominole, and P. Siegel. 2005. *2003–04 National Postsecondary Student Aid Study (NPSAS:04): Undergraduate Financial Aid Estimates for 2003–04 by Type of Institution* (NCES 2005–163). Washington, DC: U.S. Department of Education, National Center for Education Statistics.

Choy, S. P., and E. F. Cataldi. 2006. *Student Financing of Graduate and First-Professional Education, 2003–04* (NCES 2006-185). Washington, DC: U.S. Department of Education, National Center for Education Statistics.

Council of Graduate Schools. 1991. *The Role and Nature of the Doctoral Dissertation: A Policy Statement.* Washington, DC: Author.

———. 2008. *Graduate Enrollment and Degrees: 1997 to 2007.* Washington, DC: Author.

Cross, K. P. 1982. *Adults as Learners.* San Francisco: Jossey-Bass.

Houle, C. 1961. *The Inquiring Mind.* Madison: University of Wisconsin Press.

Hussar, W. J., and T. M. Bailey. 2008. *Projections of Educational Statistics to 2017* (NCES 2008-078). Washington, DC: U.S. Department of Education, National Center for Educational Statistics.

Means, B., Y. Toyama, R. Murphy, M. Bakia, and K. Jones. 2009. *Evaluation of Evidence-Based Practices in Online Learning: A Meta-Analysis and Review of Online Learning Studies.* Washington, DC: U.S. Department of Education, Office of Planning, Evaluation, and Policy Development.

Merriam, S. B., and E. L. Simpson. 2000. *A Guide to Research for Teachers and Trainers of Adults,* 2nd ed. Malabar, FL: Robert E. Krieger.

National Association of College Stores. 2006. *Questions and Answers on Copyright for the Campus Community.* Oberlin, OH: Author.

Rooney, P., W. J. Hussar, M. Planty, S. Choy, G. P. Hampden-Thompson, S. Provasnik, and M. Fox. 2006. *The Condition of Education 2006* (NCES 2006-071). Washington, DC: U. S. Department of Education, National Center for Education Statistics.

Rossman, M. H., E. Fisk, and J. Roehl. 1984. *Teaching and Learning Basic Skills: A Guide for Adult Basic Education and Developmental Education Programs.* New York: Teachers College Press.

Russell, R. L. 2002. *The No Significant Difference Phenomena: A Comparative Research Annotated Bibliography on Technology for Distance Education.* Montgomery, AL: International Distance Education Certification Center.

Snyder, T. D., and C. M. Hoffman. 2003. *Digest of Educational Statistics 2002* (NCES 2003-060). Washington, DC: U.S. Department of Education, National Center for Educational Statistics.

U.S. Census Bureau. 2007. *Current Population Reports,* series P60-233, http://pubdb3.census.gov/macro/032007/perinc/new01_000.htm (released 28 August 2007).

U.S. Department of the Treasury, Internal Revenue Service. 2008. *Publication 970: Tax Benefits for Education.* Washington, DC: Author.

General Style Guides

Entries denoted with an asterisk (*) are particularly useful.

*Achtert, W. S., and J. Gibaldi. 1998. *The MLA Style Manual,* 2nd ed. New York: Modern Language Association of America.

*American Psychological Association. 2001. *Publication Manual of the American Psychological Association,* 5th ed. Washington, DC: Author.

*Campbell, W. G., and S. V. Ballou. 1990. *Form and Style: Theses, Reports, Term Papers,* 8th ed. Boston: Houghton Mifflin.

Howell, J. B. 1983. *Style Manuals of the English-speaking World: A Guide.* Phoenix, AZ: Oryx.

*Li, X., and N. B. Crane. 1996. *Electronic Style: A Handbook for Citing Electronic Information.* Medford, NJ: Information Today. Merriam-Webster's Manual for Writers and Editors. 1998. Springfield, MA: Merriam-Webster.

*Miller, C., and K. Swift. 1988. *The Handbook of Nonsexist Writing.* New York: Harper and Row.

*Modern Language Association of America. 1999. *MLA Handbook for Writers of Research Papers, Theses, and Dissertations,* 5th ed. New York: Author.

Strunk, W., and E. B. White. 1999. *The Elements of Style,* 4th ed. New York: Macmillan.

*Turabian, K. L. 1996. *A Manual for Writers of Term Papers, Theses, and Dissertations,* 6th ed. Chicago: University of Chicago Press.

*University of Chicago Press. 2003. *The Chicago Manual of Style,* 15th ed.. Chicago: Author.

U.S. Government Printing Office. 2000. *Style Manual,* rev. ed. Washington, DC: Author.

Guides to Writing a Proposal, Thesis, Dissertation, or Research Paper

Entries denoted with an asterisk (*) are particularly useful.

*Balian, E. S. 1994. *The Graduate Research Guidebook: A Practical Approach to Doctoral/Masters Research.* Lanham, MD: University Press of America.

Barzun, J., and H. Graff. 1992. *The Modern Researcher,* 5th ed. Orlando, FL: Harcourt Brace Jovanovich.

*Behling, J. H. 1984) *Guidelines for Preparing the Research Proposal,* rev. ed. Lanham, MD: University of America Press.

*Castetter, W. B., and R. S. Heisler. 1977. *Developing and Defending a Dissertation Proposal.* Philadelphia: University of Pennsylvania, Graduate School of Education, Center for Field Studies.

Davis, G. B., and C. Parker. 1997. *Writing the Doctoral Dissertation: A Systematic Approach,* 2nd ed. Woodbury, NY: Barron's Educational Services.

Gardner, D. C., and G. J. Beatty. 1980. *Dissertation Proposal Guidebook: How to Prepare a Research Proposal and Get It Accepted.* Springfield, IL: Charles C Thomas.

*Gates, J. K. 1994. *Guide to the Use of Libraries and Information Sources,* 7th ed. New York: McGraw-Hill.

Leedy, P. D. 2001. *Practical Research: Planning and Design,* 7th ed. Upper Saddle River, NJ: Prentice Hall.

*Lincoln Y. S., and E. G. Guba. 1985. *Naturalistic Inquiry.* Beverly Hills, CA: Sage.

*Locke, L. F., W. W. Spirduso, and F. J. Silverman. 1999. *Proposals That Work: A Guide for Planning Dissertations and Grant Proposals,* 4th ed. Newbury Park, CA: Sage.

*Madsen, D. 1991. *Successful Dissertations and Theses,* 2nd ed. San Francisco: Jossey-Bass.

*Norusis, M. J. 1988. *The SPSS Guide to Data Analysis for SPSS/PC.* Chicago: SPSS.

*Powers, R. L. 1997. *Getting What You Came For: The Smart Student's Guide to Earning a Master's or a PhD,* rev. ed. New York: Noonday.

*Slade C. 2000. *Form and Style: Research Papers, Reports, and Theses.* Boston: Houghton Mifflin.

*Simon, M., and J. B. Francis. 1998. *The Dissertation Cookbook.* Dubuque, IA: Kendall/Hunt.

*University of Michigan, Horace H. Rackham School of Graduate Studies. 1990. *Dissertation Handbook: Preparing and Submitting Your Doctoral Dissertation.* Ann Arbor: Author.

*Walker, M. 1997. *Writing Research Papers: A Norton Guide,* 4th ed. New York: Norton.

*Weidenborner, S., and D. Caruso. 1994. *Writing Research Papers: A Guide to the Process,* 4th ed. New York: St. Martin.

Williams, J. M. 1990. *Style: Toward Clarity and Grace.* Chicago: University of Chicago Press.

Researching and Writing in the Disciplines

American Chemical Society. 1986. *The ACS Style Guide: A Manual for Authors and Editors.* Washington, DC: Author.

American Institute of Biological Sciences. 1978. *Council of Biological Editors Style Manual: A guide for Authors, Editors, and Publishers in the Biological Sciences,* 4th ed. Arlington, VA: Author.

American Institute of Physics. 1978. *Style Manual for Guidance in the Preparation of Papers for Journals Published by the American Institute of Physics,* 3rd ed. New York: Author.

American Medical Association. 1966. *Style Book and Editorial Manual,* 4th ed. Chicago: Author.

Barrass, R. 1978. *Students Must Write: A Guide to Better Writing for Scientists, Engineers, and Students.* New York: Wiley.

*Becker, H. S. 1986. *Writing for Social Scientists: How to Start and Finish Your Thesis, Book, or Article.* Chicago: University of Chicago Press.

Blalock, H. M. 1985. *Causal Models in the Social Sciences.* Hawthorne, NY: Aldine.

Brownlee, K. A. 1984. *Statistical Theory and Methodology: In Science and Engineering,* 2nd ed. New York: Wiley.

Campbell, D. T. 1988. *Methodology and Epistemology for Social Science: Selected Papers.* (E. S. Overman, ed.) Chicago: University of Chicago Press.

*Kerlinger, F. N. 1986. *Foundations of Behavioral Research,* 3rd ed. New York: Holt, Rinehart, and Winston.

*Krathwohl, D. R. 1988. *How to Prepare a Research Proposal for Funding and Dissertations in the Social Sciences.* Syracuse, NY: Syracuse University Press.

Kronick, D. A. 1985. *The Literature of the Life Sciences: Reading, Writing, Research.* Philadelphia: ISI [Institute for Scientific Information] Press.

Long, T. J., J. J. Convey, and A. R. Chwalek. 1985. *Completing Dissertations in Behavioral Sciences and Education: A Systematic Guide for Graduate Students.* San Francisco: Jossey-Bass.

*Morgan, J. L. 1983. *Beyond Method: Strategies for Social Research.* Beverly Hills, CA: Sage.

Remington, R., and M. A. Schork. 1985. *Statistics with Applications in the Biological and Health Sciences,* 2nd ed. Upper Saddle River, NJ: Prentice Hall.

*Smith, R. 1990. *Graduate Research: A Guide for Students in the Sciences,* 2nd ed. New York: Plenum.

INDEX

ABOUT THE AUTHOR

Dr. **Mark H. Rossman** has been advising graduate students for his entire academic career of more than forty years. He is professor emeritus at Capella University and has also served Capella University as vice president for academic affairs and associate vice president for residencies. He has served as professor and chair of education at Walden University; National Specialization Lecturer and dissertation advisor at Nova Southeastern University; professor of education and director of graduate studies at Ottawa University; associate professor of adult learning and head of the Department of Higher and Adult Education at Arizona State University; and assistant professor and head of adult education at the University of Massachusetts. He has served as a visiting scholar at the University of Kent in Canterbury, England, and at the University of Salzburg (Austria). He has chaired doctoral dissertation committees and master's thesis committees for more than 180 graduates and has served on 450-plus graduate committees. His graduates have received recognition for outstanding dissertations at Capella University, Nova Southeastern University, and Walden University. He has received two awards as an outstanding dissertation advisor. Among his other honors and awards are the Distinguished Service Award from the Commission on Adult Basic Education, a Certificate of Commendation from the Mountain Plains Adult Education Association, a Fellowship from the Salzburg Seminar in American Studies, and a Master of Humane Letters honorary degree. He is the author or coauthor of nine books, ten evaluative reports, and forty-three chapters or articles. He has produced one film, nine self-contained instructional modules, and two audiovisual tape curriculum units. He has served on the editorial boards of four professional associations and has presented ninety-one papers in fifteen states and twelve countries.